How To Be Lucky

How To Be Lucky

From teenage homeless hostel to successful
entrepreneur

A guide to making things happen

Matt Kinsella

www.mattkinsella.com

www.mattkinsella.com

First published in Great Britain by Matthew Kinsella 2011

A CIP catalogue record for this book is available from the British Library

ISBN 978-1-4477-4547-1

Printed and bound by Lulu.com

Dedications

Quite a few dedications, so many have had a hand in my great journey I wanted to say a big thanks to those people.

Firstly the biggest thanks to my wife Adrienn who really encouraged me to finish this book and made me confront my past to make something of it.

A big thanks to my Dad Clive, we have had a rocky relationship but in the last few years I could not have continued at times without your long phone chats to encourage me when things were stacked against me. The best coach/corner-man I could ask for.

Thanks to my Mum Alison who always helps me when I ask.

To my daughters Lily and Lorna I love you both very much. I had you in mind many times when writing this book, when I am not around to guide you hopefully you can find some guidance and inspiration from me in my writing.

Graham Russell thanks for starting off the thought process that eventually got me writing all this down. We have been mates for well over twenty years now and I appreciate it.

To my few close friends, old and new that have stuck by me through everything and put up with my crazy ideas, long chats and silly jokes.

I have to give some thanks to the staff and anyone involved in helping homeless people in hostels and charities around the world. I really don't know which direction my life would have gone if I had not had some guidance and care at a time when I needed it most.

Last but not least this book is dedicated to all those that find themselves homeless, not just the obvious ones you see on the street but the anonymous homeless who find circumstances conspire against them, especially the young. There is always hope, I found myself in a homeless hostel for teenagers twice but I still made it. If I can do it, you can do it!

Introduction

I am sorry if I am about to disappoint you right at the beginning but I am not going to start this book (like so many others) with statements like "I am a multi billionaire, I fly around in my own fleet of helicopters and private jets, follow my step by step instructions and you can live my lifestyle too".

I want to clarify that I don't see my goals in amounts of money, I set myself challenges, spot opportunities and pursue a better lifestyle. For example I don't want to work for someone else because I want more freedom, pride and dignity, I want to only work twenty five hours a week (or whenever I want to) so I can spend more time with my friends and family even if it means forfeiting some earnings. Of course I have made some nice money along the way and it helps but I firmly stick by "work to live, don't live to work". My story started at one of the lowest points someone can start from and my motivation was a better life and lifestyle, not money. I am what is sometimes termed a lifestyle entrepreneur, someone who is interested in happiness and rewards other than just financial ones. This is not a get rich quick book, however I do believe it contains the easiest way to achieve success and wealth with little or no backing. Whatever your goals are you can get a lot from this book, it is not just for those that want to make a lot of money but I hope you will do that too.

One other thing I want to preface the rest of this book with is this: Just because you read something here (or hear something in your daily life) that you don't like, that doesn't mean it isn't true. Try to stay open minded and absorb all you see and hear.

I actually started writing this book about four years ago but found myself writing a generic self help guide that I had read many versions of. I lost interest, thinking that nobody would want to read a book that had already been written many times by different people, so I left it on the back burner for a while. It was only when I revisited the idea that it struck me immediately what it was that I wanted to help people with. During the years since first starting the book I have spent a lot of time recognising and questioning a common issue over and over again: Why don't people see and take the hundreds of opportunities that come their way all the time in the same way that I do?

I see people letting opportunities pass them by every day; often they even see the opportunity but still let it go. I have spent time pointing out someone else's opportunity to them and tried to persuade them to take it, even though there was nothing in it for me, just the satisfaction of helping someone recognise and grasp a great opportunity, but still they won't take it. They usually have a lot of excuses and I have been frustrated so many times watching people walk away from life changing chances.

I love the saying "Right time, right place!" It's a very true and apt saying for how most wealthy people came about their fortune. There is a huge BUT though; they recognised and took the opportunities presented to them. "Right time, right place" situations happen all the time but the person or persons present don't recognise them so they walk away from their chance of good fortune. Frighteningly this happens every day. Don't let yourself be one of those that walked away from a life changing opportunity, I hope after reading this book you will not only see those chances but create some too.

If you want further information, guidance or help while reading this book (or afterwards) look up my blog/website http://mattkinsella.com I welcome any feedback or questions you have. Be Lucky.

Luck

Luck, Chance, fortune, opportunity, solutions, irons in the fire, opening, prospect, a break, dealt a good hand, benefit, opportunism, possibility, fluke, a favour, encounter.

1. My Story

I wasn't sure whether to put this part of the book at the beginning because even to me it sounds a little unbelievable and in many respects it didn't happen to the person I am now, it happened to me as I was a long time ago. Actually when I look back it seems like it happened to someone else entirely. I did not want people to think I was selling a dream "look what I did, you could do the same!" As I mentioned in the introduction when I first started writing this book I saw myself writing a cliché self help, get rich quick book and that's not what I wanted to achieve. I briefly even contemplated leaving this part out altogether but it highlights exactly how I had my eyes opened to opportunities that arise every day and how to grab them, so it made sense to put it at the beginning.

It was very hard for me to say in public and it's been a bit of a personal secret until recently. Writing it down is much easier than saying it so here it is: When I was nineteen I lived in a hostel for homeless teenagers. You can't dress that up or state it any other way, it's a very cold and sobering fact and my life was very strange for such a young person.

Today I am very proud of what I have achieved but for a long time I was very ashamed of my past, it troubled me deeply and I hardly ever discussed it. Most people would probably have been fine with it and been interested to hear about my life, but in my head I believed everyone would look down on me. I thought I was a fraud and I didn't belong in my new life so I should keep quiet if I didn't want to be found out. I spent many years since the time in the hostel never talking about it and denying it to myself to block it out, pretending I was always the person I am now. I also did not want to hurt or embarrass my family who I get on very well with now.

It was my wife that helped me talk about it more, to forgive the people (including myself) who got me into that situation and ultimately to help me finish this book. It has also been inspirational to me to remember how I turned my life around in a very short space of time and learnt some things which have helped me hugely ever since.

With no financial help, with no money at all in fact, no experience, no influential friends or relatives, I managed to totally and radically make a new life for myself. I still have very few qualifications but I make really good money, I rarely work more than 20 hours a week (because I choose to spend time with my family rather than chase more money). This is a far cry from my horrible room in the hostel where I was depressed and lonely; I drank too much, smoked too much and regularly took recreational drugs. I am living proof that anyone from any background can achieve great things and make great changes to their life.

There are a lot of reasons why people end up with nowhere to go and having experienced it myself I would never judge anyone in that situation. The reason I was homeless for a time as a very young man was simply a clash of personalities at home and a stubbornness on both sides to deal with it. As things went on I was too proud or unsure of how to ask for help.

At nineteen years old I had nothing; no proper home, no direction, no qualifications and for a while it felt like no hope either. I initially lived in my car for a short time which for such a young person is quite lonely and challenging. Sleeping in a car is not actually very easy, if you have ever tried it you will know what I mean. You can't stretch out and I'm quite tall so it was not easy, especially surrounded by plastic bags full of my stuff. Another strong memory of that time is being hungry and I mean really hungry and not being able to just pop to the fridge or run to the shops because you literally have no money. Feeling lonely and isolated was also a common theme for me at that time.

Visiting friends in high security prisons and witnessing a lot of illegal activity created some strong feelings and emotions that together with my own encouragement to go and get something better shaped me forever. It was tough at the time but looking back it was worth it and I wouldn't change it now. I see people who come from great backgrounds with a university education struggling to make sense of things that are as clear as day to me because of what I have been through, so I am happy to have endured it and become a better person from it.

2. Luck

I now understand and believe that there are two kinds of luck; the first being the kind of luck that is the bolt out of the blue type that lets someone win the lottery or blesses a couple with a baby against all odds after years of trying and failed IVF treatment. This is the kind of luck we have no control over, it just randomly bestows itself on someone, an act of God some might call it. We should be thankful for any of this luck that flows our way but we can't count on it, it's completely random.

This random luck used to be the only type of luck I thought existed and probably how most people perceive chance and luck. In the last few years I have realised that I have been personally using the second type of luck for some time, I just didn't realise it. The kind of luck you make for yourself, the chances and opportunities that we make happen ourselves. We can't go through our lives waiting for something to happen to us. Well we can but not much is going to occur except the usual mundane dross that happens to the next person. It's worth mentioning here that these days I never buy a lottery ticket because I know that the odds are far more favourable to spend that money and time on investing in the real world and creating my own good luck with it.

The other young people that I shared some time with in the hostel were very bright and sharp young men and women. You do not end up in the situation we were in without having to grow up quite quickly and being very streetwise. However looking back now I can see that stark differences opened up between us the moment I started making some life changing decisions, spotted opportunities, made some luck and worked towards my goals. It's a shame I am not in touch with any of them now. They were literally only waiting for something to happen to them, whilst I was making things happen.

Looking back throughout my life I can now see a very common theme: I have been making things happen whilst those around me have been going through the motions, generally waiting for something to happen whilst moaning about their life.

Only recently did I realise how I made things happen for myself. When I first found myself at the hostel and after things had settled down, I admit I expected something or someone to come along and give me a break, so I waited and got into all kinds of trouble while I did so. I haven't always found it easy at other crossroads in my life; I have found myself waiting for something to happen to me at various times. Luckily I have the ability to recognise these times and snap myself out of it. Just a few years ago I was tempted back into employment by a very good offer but ended up working at an awful job. I went in every day, hated almost every minute and moaned about it to myself and anyone else that would listen. I was hoping something would change and I wondered when I would be free of this depressing situation. I wasn't doing much about it though, occasionally I would look for other work but only half heatedly. I was waiting for something to just turn up, it sounds ridiculous now when I look at it but so many people are doing the same thing right now. Millions and millions of us are just existing and waiting for something to happen to us.

For a long time I thought that the kind of luck I had at nineteen, the powerful change that kicked me into action and got me a better life was the act of God type of luck. I said this to a good friend of mine a few years ago and described just how lucky I had been. His reaction really startled me, he was incredibly upset with me and disagreed quite angrily. He had obviously given my situation some thought before. He was in fact one of the few people that knew of my previous circumstances because I consciously kept it private from most people. He told me quite forcefully that I had made my own luck, that I recognised opportunities when they presented themselves and I took full advantage of them. He was also convinced that I could recognise even the slimmest of half chances and make them into something. He was angry with me for not giving myself enough credit and he pointed out how so many people blindly wait for something to happen to them and miss opportunities that pass right in front their noses all the time. That conversation was the initial inspiration and foundation of this book.

Since that chat I spent a long time considering my experiences and what I had seen other people do (or not do). Now I can really see that there actually is a second kind of luck; the luck we make for ourselves. I didn't have any training in making the most of these opportunities, nobody even pointed it out to me until years after I started doing it. It's not a difficult thing to do either, with the right attitude and understanding you can open your eyes to all the opportunities there are available to help you that you never saw before.

Something I have realised is that one person may view a particular problem as dire and insurmountable, whilst someone else might look at that same issue as nothing and everyday life to them. Everything is relative to each individual. No challenge or problem is insurmountable, things may not work out exactly as we want them to and we may need to adapt as the challenge evolves but problems can be overcome. So many opportunities are out there; our dreams and goals can be achieved.

As I sat in my room at the teenage homeless hostel at nineteen years old I felt like my situation could not be worse. I was convinced that my life was set to be that crap forever and I could not see a way out; my problems seemed insurmountable. My own view of my situation at that time was awful, I was under no illusions whatsoever and I had very little hope.

I went through a period of blaming everyone for where I was; my family, where I grew up, my friends, the education system and myself, the list goes on. I think I blamed everyone and everything at some point. This changed when I made the one decision that changed my life. With a massive determination and conviction I would change my life for the better. I recognised the hole I was in and I suddenly saw that I was making it worse. By blaming everyone else, by wallowing in the problems I had, getting up at midday and moping around I was making everything worse. I decided I could change my life right then and there; I suddenly realised I could make massive changes straight away.

I think it would do everyone some good to hit rock bottom (and I mean rock bottom) with nothing, because there is no greater inspiration to get yourself together and realise your full potential. This is because you have nothing to lose, you will grab every chance no matter how small or how embarrassing, you don't have any pride so you will do almost anything. Also if you have been at rock bottom, for the rest of your life you will never be afraid to take chances because you will know you can lose everything and still make it back. You never have anything to lose. I didn't realise it at the time but I had made a conscious decision to start creating some opportunities for myself, start making some of my own good luck; I was learning how to be lucky.

The first goal seemed so massive to me at the time that I couldn't see beyond it. Some self help books I have read say you have to set yourself many goals and paths to achieving them straight away and work out a structured route to your dreams. I can't always accept this process because for me, at that time, I was so low and clinically depressed. Sitting down and working out a whole load of goals and steps would have been impossible and would have only compounded thoughts I had of not being capable of pushing myself out of the situation I was in. I didn't think about any of this long and hard at the time, I literally woke up one day and decided that my life wasn't good enough. I said to myself that my situation was not acceptable; I wanted much more than a crappy room in a hostel. I wanted a house, a nice car, foreign holidays and a family to enjoy it all with. I decided "WHATEVER it takes", that is what I am going to achieve. I remember repeating it to myself over and over "whatever it takes, whatever it takes". These thoughts and decisions took a few minutes at the most but it was the most life changing experience I have had and was the start of something huge.

I knew had to get a job, not just any job, I wanted something that would give me a leg up out of the mess I was in. I already had a part time job at a local supermarket, if I really wanted to I could have worked full time there but that wasn't good enough. I hated working at that place, I was treated like a number and an undervalued asset. I was chastised for the smallest mistakes and poorly paid, minimum wage did not exist where I was at that time. Worst of all I was treated like a robot that could be used as they wished and my thoughts and opinions counted for nothing, which for an intelligent person is hard to take. Even if the money was better it would not have been good enough.

As the first few days went by I felt more and more determined. I have heard and read about entrepreneurs and athletes with the huge determination they have. I don't think you can just magic up that kind of determination. This is one of the problems with depression and having lows in your life, you cannot just "pull yourself together", it doesn't work like that. The human mind doesn't operate like this; if you are in a rut you can't just tell yourself to "sort it out!" Determination grows from an idea and your own enthusiasm.

As I started making small steps towards my goal of a new career the determination and enthusiasm within me grew until it was a full blown conviction. Add a large amount of belief to that enthusiasm and it's amazing what you can do even if you are down and out. I think the year that I spent in the hostel gave me time to reflect and build my confidence to go out and achieve something. It's amazing how we don't give ourselves more time to think, reflect and build our confidence to move on to the next challenge. I wonder if a lot of people suffering from depression gave themselves time without pressure and got quality counselling, would they really need medication? We are often too hard on ourselves and push ourselves into things too quickly. Time really is a great healer.

I set about getting a new career as if it was my actual job. I remember thinking very clearly that I had decided "my job is to get a job" and to tackle it in the same way as going to work every day. I committed to getting up every day at 7.30am, have a shower, shave and iron a shirt. I would work Monday to Friday, 9.00am to 6.00pm until I had secured my new career. It changed my mind set, it made me think differently and it immediately gave me a new sense of purpose. Just doing this every day made me happier.

These days you can go into most libraries or an Internet cafe and sit down at a computer for very little money or for free. It was 1997 and computers were around but not like now, so I had to be creative to get my CV/resume typed and printed. I went straight to the careers office in my local town and talked them into letting me use their computer and printer. They didn't advertise the fact that they let people type up their CVs/resumes there and they didn't make a habit of it but I started to realise very quickly that if you are polite and (more importantly) really enthusiastic, most people genuinely want to help you. The lady in the office liked my enthusiasm so much that she let me dictate what I wanted in my CV/resume and she typed it for me. I also got a few copies printed off for free in exchange for some more enthusiasm and a smile, and then I set about looking for some jobs.

Before and since then I have never been afraid to ask for small favours. What's the worst that can happen? They say no and you ask someone else who will say yes. I recognise now this is all part of being lucky or creating good luck; just ask.

I vaguely remember a few years ago watching a TV documentary about different personality types. The one part of this series that stuck in my mind was a timed challenge they set for the different personality types, divided into group according to type. They had to go to a supermarket, buy the ingredients for a spaghetti bolognese, go back to a house and cook it all in the fastest time possible. As part of the challenge the TV crew closed the aisle with the pasta in using cones and a safety barrier to see how the different teams reacted to this problem. One group would not cross the barrier at all; they obeyed the no entry sign and failed the challenge. Another group hesitated for a long time and discussed the issue at length. They eventually decided to cross the barrier and get the pasta to complete the challenge, but it cost them a lot of time. The final team of the psychological type that make up most entrepreneurs did not take any notice of the barrier and no entry signs; it was as if it wasn't there and they won the challenge hands down. I love this example of how rules are just made to be broken if you want to get what you want. Don't worry about what you should do, do what you have to do (within reason, don't hurt anyone).

My location during my time in the hostel was in a very backward and rundown south coast seaside area, I won't embarrass the area by naming it but at that time it was not the easiest place to find work in anything other than a shop, hotel or fishing boat. However I was incredibly determined to find something office based; I had decided this was the way to a better life. I'm not sure why I decided that because I hate working in an office now and escape outside or somewhere more interesting whenever I can these days.

I had heard on the grapevine that they were offering some reasonable apprenticeships in various places near to where I lived. Although they were not offering great salaries it was good "on the job" training, a foot on the ladder and a start to my CV/resume. As I didn't have any real qualifications or experience this seemed like my best bet. I started by studying all the job sections in the local newspapers and almost straight away found an advertisement for a trainee admin/IT person. It sounded perfect; IT was the future and I had used a computer a few times. How hard could it be? I made a phone call and got an interview arranged in a few days' time.

The first problem I panicked about was not having anything to wear. Living in a homeless hostel your suit and tie collection tends to be a bit thin on the ground. I didn't have a suit when I made the decision "my job is to get a job" and I couldn't afford one either. I mentioned my situation and what I was trying to achieve quietly to one of the hostel staff and they suggested if I needed a suit I should check out the charity shops.

I had never even been in a charity shop at that point in my life and I thought I would be ridiculed by my peers for just wearing a suit, let alone one I had bought in a charity shop. I didn't let that stop me though, I was so determined; solutions kept presenting themselves to me and I just had to accept them. I went to a few different charity shops and explained to them what I was doing and that I needed a suit. They had a massive range of suits, shirts and ties that had hardly been worn, kindly donated by people. I used all the change in my pocket to pay for a really nice suit and tie! It fitted perfectly and looked as though it was made for me.

I took some big steps to accept solutions that seemed strange to me and to do something that I had never done before, which I could have been ridiculed for. How many times have we not done something for these reasons? Later in life especially, people tend to not follow certain paths because they are too new and untested or because they could be shunned by their peers. I have started to follow my own example more and more lately and it's working, I can highly recommend it; do something totally random that you would like to do but you are not sure about to prove you are still alive, it's great.

On the day of the big interview I got up nice and early, ironed my suit, got my CV/resume together, got some notepaper and pen and gave myself plenty of time to make the forty minute walk to where the interview was. This is where I got taught the most valuable lesson of my life, at that place, at that time I was shown/taught by myself (by accident) how to make things happen. I got to the office building nice and early and what I didn't understand at the time was that many office buildings, even small ones, often have more than one company inside. I went up to the reception and explained I was there for an interview. Immediately the receptionist said "OK, no problem I know who you are here to see, take a seat". I waited for the interviewer to come down and eventually a young guy came down to collect me.

I was lead to the interview room and introduced to two gentlemen and one lady and as they started talking to me it quickly dawned on me that I was in the wrong interview! The woman was not the woman I had spoken to on the phone and was not who I was supposed to be speaking to. My heart sank and I was a little embarrassed but they were talking to me about an IT job and they were keen to talk to me even though they seemed a little puzzled about who I was and I think they mentioned perhaps the agency had sent me without passing on the details to them.

At this point I could have just said sorry, I'm in the wrong place. Manners and etiquette dictate that's what I should have done; there was a woman downstairs at another company expecting me and I shouldn't be wasting these people's time. However I didn't. I just decided to see if I could get through the interview without them knowing and even see if they liked me enough to offer me a job. It's crazy actually and I don't fully know why I did it, I was incredibly nervous and embarrassed but I hid it well and soldiered on through the interview.

The company was an IT training business, it was quite a young business but doing well and expanding rapidly. I just threw at them all the enthusiasm and positive attitude I had built up over the last two weeks and it worked. I know for a certain fact that everyone I know, if put in the same situation would have done one of two things: they would have apologised for coming to the wrong place and found the right company or they would have been struck with embarrassment, said as little as possible, left and gone home with their tail between their legs.

I could see straight away they were offering a better position than the half a job I was supposed to be going for and I thought: Why not? I'm here, I can do this! Admittedly I had to lie quite a bit in the interview: "Can you install different operating systems and quickly configure them for use in a training environment?" they asked, "oh yes no problem at all" I replied "I grew up with different computers at home so I could manage that" I was telling half the truth. The reality was my Dad brought home a couple of computers from work and my brother (who was the true IT enthusiast) spent hours messing around with them and I occasionally played a game on them or watched him sometimes whilst calling him a nerd.

Embarrassing yourself by going to the wrong interview is not what most people would consider an opportunity but it was and that is what I soon realised. Opportunities are everywhere but we discard them and run away from them. For various reasons we don't see these master strokes of luck; embarrassment in this case, other times laziness, fear, too shy to ask for help, low confidence, manners or it's not the done thing and many other reasons people give themselves for not grabbing an opportunity.

I went home after that interview a little confused as to what happened but also with some pride that they seemed to like me and maybe, just maybe, they might offer me the job. There was also a part of me that thought I was a total idiot and only I could go to the wrong interview and nobody could get a job by going to the wrong interview.

The next day I got a call on the pay phone in the hostel, luckily the pay phone was on the wall just outside my room so I was able to grab the phone before any of the other loons got to it.

It was from the IT training company and I had got the job! I couldn't contain my joy at all, I was over the moon and I remember crying because I was so happy. They explained they were about to move offices to a bigger premises and when that move was complete in about four to five weeks they wanted me to start. That suited me perfectly because it gave me a month or so to work on all the things I said I could do but actually could not do.

Here is another good point; I have never turned down or let an opportunity go by because of a tiny reason like not knowing anything about whatever is being asked. If you have half a brain almost anything can be learned quite quickly, certainly enough to get by and learn the rest as you go.

Maybe it was my age and naivety at the time but I never felt like I couldn't achieve something. I didn't present myself with excuses not to do something. I only saw possibilities and my mind worked overtime to think of ways and shortcuts to make them happen. As I have got a little older I have heard so many excuses from people (including myself sometimes) not to do something. "I don't have enough financial backing, I have asthma, I come from the wrong background, I don't have any qualifications, I'm too old, I'm too young" and the list goes on.

It is very stupid and none of it is true, we can achieve almost anything.

When I was eight years old I hated school, something no eight year old should feel so early in their life. I was told constantly in class that I was lazy and that I should work harder. I was always being made to stay in the classroom at lunch time and during P.E. so I could catch up with work I was falling behind with. No matter how hard I tried I could not keep up with writing and reading in class. Every parents evening was the same and I would dread my parents coming home and reciting the terrible reports my teachers had discussed with them.

On one such parent's evening just before my ninth birthday my father was listening to yet another terrible description of his "lazy" son from one of my teachers and he said "this just doesn't sound like my son". He came home and asked me what was going on. I must have said something that made him think because he looked into educational problems in children and took me to see an educational psychologist. I spent almost an entire day doing tests and exercises whilst various people took notes. The result was I had a higher than average IQ with an excellent memory but I was also diagnosed with a form of dyslexia. I was very self conscious about this diagnosis at first and dyslexia was quite a new, controversial condition at the time.

I didn't really discuss it with anyone and after a while it didn't really faze me either. I just initially had a hope that my school life would get better and that I would get some kind of support from my teachers and the school. My parents felt the same but we were wrong, my teachers never fully understood the condition and never gave me any slack because of it. Despite what my parents and I felt at the time this was the best outcome for me because I managed to cope, never used it as an excuse and I hardly even consider it now. It does occasionally cause me some frustration and at times it really pisses me off but I deal with it, I adapt and find ways to cope, it's not a major problem for me at all. I never discuss it with anyone because they don't need to know and I refuse to use it as an excuse.

I do not crave any sympathy for my problems or extra credit for issues I have overcome. Everyone has problems, everyone has adversities they have to overcome to achieve new things. Amazing individuals win marathons in wheelchairs, people who can't speak achieve great academic success and every day someone with much greater difficulties than you or I achieves the most amazing feats that we will not manage to do in our lifetime. Never make excuses not to even attempt something. People make excuses and blame others for their problems every day. To change and lead a fulfilling life you can't make excuses or blame others for everything that is wrong with your life. Recognise who you are and be glad for who you are.

If we make a conscious decision to make changes and do something different as we move forward we will not see problems or make excuses, solutions and answers to issues will present themselves to us and we will use them. If opportunities and solutions are not forthcoming we can actively seek them, create them and implement them.

In seeking solutions for myself I was starting to realise that you can ask for opportunities. If you are enthusiastic and polite people are really willing to help you. A recent survey was done that asked managers whether they would consider giving the majority of their staff a pay rise if they asked for it, the overwhelming answer from those managers was yes, not for all the staff but they would consider it for most of their staff. In the same survey employees were questioned whether they had ever asked their boss for a raise and the overwhelming answer from them was no they had not. This proves that often all we need to do to get some of the things we want or need is to simply ask. We don't ask enough, sometimes even if there isn't someone to ask I often just ask for something from myself or from the world, a bit like a prayer. I know it sounds nuts but strangely it works. If you don't ask you don't get! Don't forget to say thanks too when you get what you wanted.

I decided to test this theory and my new found confidence after I had been offered that job by asking someone for a big favour. I had met this guy just once about one year previously and sometimes I am surprised how bold and unembarrassed I was but at the time I didn't care and I had to ask, so I did. Craig was an IT manager at a private hospital in London and I met him briefly when he visited near where I was living and he popped in to see my dad. I needed some work experience to get up to speed before I started my new job and he seemed like the only person to ask. I made a few phone calls and managed to track down his phone number.

I called him up and explained I had a job offer but I wasn't sure how much of the job I could do, I was pretty honest with him. I asked him if I could work in his department for one month for free; I could learn what I needed to know and he got a free pair of hands for a month. Thankfully he agreed and he was so taken with my enthusiasm that he even invited me to stay in his spare room for the month. This was great because I had got so carried away with the idea of going up to London for a month I hadn't even considered where I was going to stay.

I really made this opportunity happen for myself; nobody was going to offer me work experience or help to train me up to the standard I would need to pull off the job I had just landed. Only my own initiative, enthusiasm, ideas and confidence got me that work experience. If Craig had said no I would have asked around until I got something, I was that determined. I know a lot of people would have sat around for a month, maybe gone to the library a few times for some IT books and just waited for the job to start but I was on a roll and I could just make things happen and it was great. I loved it.

As we get older we build up more inhibitions and I include myself in this. I have to break down the inhibitions I have built up over the last fifteen years and be more open, honest and unafraid to ask for things as I did at nineteen. It works, it worked for me then and it's working for me now. If you confidently, humbly and graciously ask people for their help with something that they can easily do for you and as long as it doesn't put them out too much, they usually oblige quite happily.

In today's society we are often too scared to speak to our own neighbours! Don't be, talk to everyone, no matter what they look like or where you might meet them; it's always nice to make new friends and you never know when you might need them. Don't limit yourself to people on the same social, economic or educational level. Everyone has something to offer it's usually someone very different or foreign to you that you can get the most from, and they can get even more from you.

I have made really useful contacts in the most random places. Strangely enough the worst places I have found for making contacts are business clubs designed specifically to encourage networking and to make contacts. These places are often very "forced" affairs where everyone feels pressure to network and you can feel very self conscious. Better networking clubs do exist now and in fact a great friend of mine started a very good one based on her similarly bad experiences and her determination to create something better.

Whenever you meet someone that you get along with, it doesn't take much to go the extra mile to encourage further contact; don't wait for them to ask for your contact details and suggest meeting up again, you should do it. People like to help others, it makes us feel good about ourselves. We also like to see others succeed, those that don't are not worth wasting our time with and there is always someone else who will help. Don't forget to return the favour when someone asks you for some assistance that you could easily help them with. Even if they might not have anything to offer you, if they are politely asking for something you could easily help with, do it, it will come back to you at some point from someone or something.

My first week in London was a little overwhelming to be honest. The underground trains, the very early starts and the work was quite hard. My new temporary colleagues didn't hold back because I was only doing one month's work experience, they expected me to work hard; I was often doing eleven hours plus every day. I enjoyed myself too though; the hospital staff liked to play hard as well as work hard and regularly stopped in the pub between the office and the tube station on the way home from work. I learned after a while that burning the candle at both ends was a bad idea but it took me a while to figure that out and I had fun trying to find a way to manage it.

I really made the most of that month, I learned a lot but also tried extra hard to pull my weight to repay Craig for giving me the chance and letting me stay at his place. When the month was up I got a call from the IT training company back home to say it would be another two weeks before I could start my new job. I went straight to Craig's office and asked if I could stay on another two weeks, still free of charge until I started my new job. He quickly said "No". I was a bit disappointed but was ready to say "thanks anyway" when he said "Come and work here, we are about to embark on a huge project, you work hard and we could use you". I was stunned and unsure what to say at first but it didn't take long for me to like the idea. "I can offer you more than the IT training company are going to pay and you can stay at mine until you find a place of your own" Craig offered and how could I say no.

From going to the wrong interview to landing a great job in London in just a couple of months was incredible but I made it happen by seizing and creating the opportunities I was presented with. I am not special; anyone with the right enthusiasm and attitude could do the same. YOU could do the same!

3. The Right People

This luck that took me from homeless hostel to IT job in London was not a one off in my life and despite some hiccups and some occasional procrastinating, I have followed similar principals since with great results. An important tip I can give is to surround yourself with like-minded people; you will all help each other in different ways and everyone will benefit at some point. Since Craig helped me all those years ago I have been there for him during difficult times and vice versa too, Craig is like family to me now.

Cultivate those relationships that you know will be good for you and don't waste time on people that are negative towards you and/or won't be helped. Waste your time and energy on the good people and you will be rewarded. I am sorry to say that there are people who will not be helped. Until I met my wife I used to think that most people (apart from the odd exceptions) were capable of very much the same things, given the right training, coaching, experience, support and time. My fantastic wife regularly points out that we are different and we have something about us that some people don't have and slowly I have understood she is right. The fact you are reading this book and keen to know more points out that you are different too.

I can see now there are most definitely people out there who will never do anything different, won't be helped, won't help themselves and will live out their lives as they are. I don't think those people would buy my book however, so they won't read this. The group of people who read this (you) are capable of great things but just need a nudge or maybe a full on shove over the line into the group of risk taking nut jobs that I belong to. I would like to point out that our group of risk taking nut jobs is also (generally speaking) the wealthiest, contented and happiest group of the lot.

A close friend of mine Matt (who was my best man) once jokingly shouted at me "you are so far over the line, the line is a dot to you" I think this is an adapted line from an episode of the TV show Friends so he can't take full credit but we laughed a lot about it because it's true. I could say the same about him and that's one reason why we are mates. We don't feel like normal society "rules" apply to us. We are not hurting anyone, we just want to be free of constraints and enjoy our lives, which we do.

Surrounding yourself with the right people is so important, I can't say this enough times. A child's friends will have a bigger impact on their school life and personality than the school they go to or their parents (no matter what you believe). It's the same when you are an adult; your friends, colleagues, contacts and acquaintances will greatly affect your potential, in good ways and in bad ways. Lose the bad friends, you know who they are, they're the ones that take but don't give back and you want them to change but deep down you know they won't.

This brings me on to a very important point; you have to be able to let things go. Friends, jobs, homes, failed businesses and the list goes on of all the things I have had to let go so I could keep moving forward. Don't cling on to something that doesn't give you anything. Some projects are slow burners but if it does not show any signs of life and you are definitely losing interest, then ditch it. Sometimes I have been quite cold but you can't waste energy on looking back all the time. If you want to stand still and keep everything the same that is fine, stop reading now, you should not be reading this book. To move forward you will inevitably have to leave some people and some things behind. I know it sounds cold but you do build up a knack of quickly moving on, you have to. I have realised there are people who will happily drag everyone down, hold you back and stop all progress. I don't have time for that, I want to move forward and help as many people (that want to be helped) as I can. The thing I realised was the people who love you, understand you and support you will always be there for you. The friendships and projects that don't work out and get left behind are just fate and they were meant to be left behind.

4. Why Don't People Recognise Opportunities?

This is a question I ask all the time and I am learning more on this every day.

I think fear is the biggest enemy of taking a chance, fear of change, fear of the unknown and a fear of risk. "Why rock the boat and make a change? I am safe and secure in my little, comfortable world, I am not happy but I am safe so I will keep it that way". If you want "safe" stop reading and give this book to someone else. Safe is boring and safe is often unhappy as well.

Some have suggested laziness but I am not sure about this because at times I can be the king of lazy. I am not afraid of hard work and I often put in long hours across so many projects, but I am not the hardest working person out there and I never will be. I think this is where and why my talent developed; I was always looking for the easier way, always. I would employ my mind and charm to find the shortest, most direct and simplest route to what I needed or wanted. This started in school and developed as I went through life and out into the world of work. So I'm not sure laziness is an issue but there are different types of laziness. A lack of motivation is not laziness.

Too polite to ask; this is one I have witnessed myself and it quite literally pisses me off. Someone is there offering something to someone else and they are too polite to take it or enquire further. When living in the hostel I lost quite a lot of dignity and I had no problems asking for anything from anyone, I had to. Since then I realised that generally people like helping other people and it's not impolite to ask for things.

We don't have our eyes fully open. We walk around blind to things most of the time. You might believe it's not nice to think "what can I get out of this situation" every time you walk in a room or meet with someone but it's honestly how most successful people think. You don't have to be rude or mercenary in the way you approach things. In fact you won't achieve much unless you are likeable; if you are and you ask in the right way most people will be happy to help even if it's just in a small way like giving you a contact or pointing you in the right direction for what you need.

What is funny is when other people point out my opportunities and say "it's alright for you, look at the opportunities open to you!" and I reply "yes and there are opportunities open to you that are not there for me so we are even, the only difference is I take my opportunities and you can see me doing it so it's easy for you to see my fortune. Stop looking at my chances and focus on your own". I am simply seeing and creating chances that are open and available to me, if I was in your shoes, in your neighbourhood and with your contacts I would be making different things happen.

5. Existing Outside of the Flock

One very important cause of people's wariness to strike out and do something different is society. Whether you like it or not you are probably a sheep and you follow what everyone else does because you feel safe doing that. There is a reason for this and it is because human beings as animals are the herding or pack type, just like dogs, sheep, horses and cows. Psychologically we feel safer doing what everyone else is doing and we feel odd to go against the flow and stand out.

This instinct is stronger in children as this is when we are most vulnerable. We all remember a time when we stood out because of something we did or had to wear at school and we hated it; we just wanted to fit in and be anonymous. We carry this through our lives and although we dream of better things we end up living in similar houses in housing developments, driving very similar cars, wearing similar clothes, all going to our jobs at the same time and coming home at the same time. This is often referred to and defined as the rat race and I spent a lot of my life trying to get as far away from the rat race as possible.

In any pack or herd there is a leader, an individual that does not feel uneasy doing what they want and going where they like, this is the one that all the others blindly follow. In pack animals you get an alpha male and female that the others follow and they all feel comfortable in their roles within the hierarchy. In herding animals like horses you similarly get individuals that are independent and are happy to lead the others; in elephants a matriarch will lead the others to the best watering holes and feeding grounds. Human beings deep down in our natural instincts are essentially the same, some are leaders but most just feel comfortable being lead. This doesn't mean that someone who is lead can't become a leader.

Governments love these facts and use them to control the masses; the government takes the role of the leader and we blindly follow. During the cold war the Russians did this to great affect and managed to control millions of people across eastern Europe, something I am learning about first hand with my involvement in Hungary. The Chinese government do it today to try to control over a billion individuals.

The thing most of us don't realise is western governments do it too, they are just much more subtle and clever about it. By forcing us into school (a legal requirement) we are force fed propaganda every day about what society expects from us: do well in school, go to university or get further training, get a nine to five job and work hard, buy a house have a family, pay taxes and don't make a fuss. Most people don't even grasp the fact that from that first day at school we are told every day where to be and at what time and this basically carries on until we retire sixty years later! If you are told where to be and at what time every day isn't that a loss of freedom? I really don't like being told what to do and I value my freedoms a lot so these things really stand out to me.

Governments don't like individuals doing something different; they like all the "ants" out doing their allocated jobs, all controlled nicely and paying taxes to keep the machine moving. I know a lot of people will laugh at these facts but it is so obvious when you have looked from the outside in, as I did when I was in the hostel and as I do now.

There isn't anything ultra sinister about this, the governments like everybody to be conditioned or institutionalised to go to work every day without fail and pay their taxes automatically through their wages every month with minimal fuss. When men and women join the military they are given a more intense version of the same conditioning we get when we start school but it is very similar. They are told where to be at what time, what to wear and how to wear it, what time lunch is and what they will eat. In the military your life is controlled and managed which suits some people but it can cause big problems when they leave. The struggles of ex military staff adjusting to civilian life is well documented, they can find it hard to cope with the enormous amount of choices they have to make just to function on a basic level. They can suddenly do whatever they want, when they want and this can be tough.

What is not well documented is something I witnessed first-hand a few times but saw it in most detail when it happened to my wife. When someone gives up the rat race, a nine to five routine and gets their freedom back they can have similar issues to someone leaving the military. I know this sounds farfetched and if I had heard this six or seven years ago I would have been interested, but would have found it hard to believe. I only accepted it after seeing it for myself. The first time I saw it happen was to a friend who was made redundant and he decided to work freelance. I worked hard with him to encourage and support him but when I wasn't around he couldn't cope with the freedom; he struggled to get up on time and motivate himself but mostly he just felt lost in the freedom of not having to be somewhere at a certain time and be told what to do. Within two months he took the first job that was offered to him. Unfortunately he bounced around a few jobs being quite unhappy after that, but I am happy to say he finally set up a print company, which today is going from strength to strength and he has never been happier.

When my wife went through something similar I really saw how it could affect someone. Adrienn, like most people, had started school young and she was a keen student, she studied further and went to university. She wasn't a natural academic but she worked hard, enjoyed it and got a good degree. She finished university at twenty four and started work soon after that. We met when she was twenty eight years of age and working for a medical company in the UK and at that point she had only spent a few weeks between jobs during her career, so she had been in nearly continuous education and employment for twenty three years.

After a year of being together it was obvious she was not very happy in her job and she saw the freedom I enjoyed so we decided we didn't need the money that badly so she should resign and spend some time thinking about what she wanted to do in the long term. It truly shocked me how quickly she felt lost without the daily routine. Within just two weeks she was telling me she had made a mistake and she should go back to the job she hated; I couldn't believe it. The point I found hard to take was that Adrienn couldn't tell me why she wanted to go back to a crappy, over worked, disrespectful job. She agreed she didn't like the people or the job, she just felt compelled to do it and go back to the nine to five routine. I tried to encourage her to do things she enjoyed and she tried to get some work as a freelance translator.

Adrienn really tried but she struggled so much too. I didn't understand it at first but after a few months I became aware that she had been institutionalised over twenty three years to follow a certain path, she had taken herself away from that path and she was way out of her comfort zone. All she wanted to do was get another job, almost anything that came along she wanted to take so she could get back into that comfort zone. I continued to encourage her, I literally begged her to give herself more time to reflect and think about what she really wanted to do in her life.

Luckily at around that time we moved house and this took her mind off things and gave her a different focus. After we moved (nine months after leaving her job) she came to me with some ideas she had for selling cosmetics and related products independently. She was passionate about it and said she would like to try but was worried it wouldn't make much money. I told her that it didn't matter how much money it made if it made her happy. After a slow start Adrienn's cosmetics business started to grow and after six months (fifteen months after leaving her job) she is doing really well, importing products directly from several different countries and selling them at shows she organises herself. I have given her almost no help with this and I am so proud of her for coming through it all. My proudest moments were when she told me several times during that period that she would never get a nine to five employed job again; she loves the freedom she has and cannot believe she wanted to go back to traditional work.

Much of western society today is a hangover from the industrial revolution which occurred only 300 years ago. Before that time human beings existed on earth for approximately 20,000 years with individual trades; being self-sufficient hunters, merchants, traders and farmers. Our ancestors existed very happily and successfully without being forced into a place of work on a daily basis or being told what to do for an amount of money chosen by someone else. They would have had a trade and worked when they had to, or chose to and set their fees at rates that suited them and their customers. Others would have had small farms and produced all that they needed to exist and produce extra to trade for additional things they required or desired. This evolution of man and humanity went on (aside from the odd invasion and revolution) for millennia with human psychology evolving with that way of life.

When the industrial revolution started the promise of a regular, secure job with a regular, stable income obviously appealed to a lot of people. The reality however is a trap, once you sign up it's very hard to go back. Once the family business or farm was sold and the life in the factory set in, with debts that needed to be serviced, it was very hard to go back. It's a trap that still exists today and I'm sure many will be familiar with the treadmill we get on today and find ourselves stuck on.

The lure more than anything, then and now, is the feeling of security in a stable and safe job. This was and still is the biggest lie. I have seen companies sailing very close to the wind, whilst still recruiting new staff, telling the whole work force what a great organisation they work for and how they should think themselves lucky to work there. Then in the next round of refinancing they can't raise the capital to service their debts and/or crippling overheads so they start laying people off. Totally out of the blue families are left struggling to pay mortgages and bills. Nobody is immune from hard times, recessions or other economic issues, but at least if you are in charge of the balance sheet you know in good time when you need to find a new strategy and you build up the skills to deal with these problems better.

Individualism has been struggling on this planet ever since the industrial revolution, but particularly in the last 150 years. During that time some of the worst atrocities committed by humanity have occurred: the holocaust in Europe, the first and second world wars, serious human rights abuses in communist countries and dictatorships, the genocide in Cambodia and the list goes on. All of which occurred because of the human nature to follow what everyone else is doing with a fear of standing out and the closely related human tendency of persecuting those that don't fit in or those that stand up against the masses.

We should go back to our real roots and I believe people will be much happier. Be yourself, stand up for who you are and rely on yourself to make things happen for you. The more we look to others for the answers, the more we will be disappointed. Our luck, fortune and future is within us, it won't come from others, from society or government. Your good luck is within you, not anyone else.

I can now see Adrienn needed that time to rehabilitate herself from the twenty three years of conditioning and institutionalising she had received from an early age. After seeing and experiencing this episode I wondered why I had never been through this and I think that my time living in the hostel and my experiences starting businesses at a young age had broken up any long cycles of conditioning, so I felt free to do whatever I wanted, without feeling worried or guilty or lost without boundaries and rules. I want everyone to know what this feels like and you can only do it by giving yourself time. Doing something different for three months is not enough; I truly believe it takes over a year to properly recondition yourself as in Adrienn's case.

Now I understand this whole thing better, I see it happening all the time; people leave their jobs or they try a new business, move abroad for a new life or whatever the big change might be and within six months to a year they are back doing the same old crap again because they didn't give themselves enough time to adjust. Don't make the same mistake, don't be afraid to try something new but give yourself time and don't be surprised if you find that following your dreams is tough at first but believe me, one day you will look back and wonder how you coped before. Don't be scared of failure; I and many other successful people have failed as often or even more often than we have succeeded, it's just the successes were bigger than the failures.

During these kinds of transitions there will be friends and ex colleagues who try to drag you back because they don't want to be reminded how boring or shitty their life is, so they don't want you to succeed and rub their noses in it. Don't let others put you off. You often need to be single minded and independent because even your closest friends can get jealous or worry you will leave them behind so they will try and put a negative spin on opportunities so you don't take them. Believe me, in the end they will respect you for your success and if they don't, you don't need those kind of people around you anyway.

I would like to add here that the reason we moved house at that time was because my wife and I were both going through a period of reflection and something we realised together was that we were only living in that area for work. We had very few real friends there, neither of our families were anywhere near that area and we didn't enjoy much about the place at all; it was purely for work we had moved and stayed there. How many of you or your friends are in that situation? Moved away for work but living a lonely life away from friends and family, feeling that they must do it because the job is good.

A job isn't someone's life, a job or career can't replace your closest friends, your partner or children. Apart from the odd exception, I challenge anyone to find true peace and happiness in their lives while being totally isolated. There is nothing I could do or buy, for any amount of money that would give me any more happiness than having fun with my friends and family. Cue the people telling me that they can't just quit a job no matter how much they don't like it and/or the place they live and go back home to their family. My answer to that is: why not? Will your family see you on the street? Even if they did I know from experience there are friends, agencies and charities that can step in if you descend that far. I can also say from experience that it takes a lot to get that far down and with enough effort it is always possible to pull things back. Can't you have some time to think of a new career path and be around your family and/or friends while you do it?

I see people I grew up with living quite happy and fulfilled lives close to their family having never moved away like I did. Don't be ashamed to admit you made a mistake and you miss your home town, closest friends and family.

Never be afraid to admit you made the wrong career choice or finally call it a day on a failing business. Do the right thing and close the door on it for your own good. You can always come back to it later if you want to.

Having some time to reflect in an environment you are most comfortable in, or even somewhere completely new to you might be all you need to come up with that amazing plan to make your first million.

6. Formula Followers

There are certain types of people I like to call "formula followers". These are the people who believed what they were told when teachers and parents said "do well in school, go to university, become a lawyer/dentist/architect and your life will be good". These youngsters set about following the formula and now they are the lawyer/dentist/architect that they and their parents dreamed they would be.

These people tend to dislike people like me because they see me with no qualifications and I didn't follow the formula, I did it the "easy way" and I have a better car, nicer house and I work less than they do. I am the person doing what they were told was impossible and it does not compute in their heads. They think I must have cheated or stolen something or I was just very lucky. When I tell them there is nothing lucky about living in a homeless hostel at a young age, you can almost see the steam coming from their ears as they struggle to make sense of my situation.

What really makes me feel sorry for the vast majority of formula followers is that eventually the truth dawns on them; after years of studying and doing what they were told, getting their university degrees and landing a reasonable first rung job (or not landing a job at all as many are out of work entirely) and working their way up a bit, they are no further forward than most other people. They earn just over average salaries, that nice big house is still not within reach, they are still flying economy class on their holidays along with everyone else and they are still struggling to pay off the credit card and so on.

Where is the life they were promised? OK, they are not sweeping streets but neither am I, or quite a few other people who didn't follow the formula. Some like me are doing even better than the formula followers, how was that allowed to happen?

Formula, structure and routine are like death and poison to creativity, happiness, enjoyment and ultimately success. Void your life of structure and routine, enjoy yourself, take in the world around you, spend time with the people that mean the most to you and you will find whatever it is you are looking for.

As I touched upon at the end of the last chapter, don't be afraid to admit you were wrong or made mistakes. Failure is never the end; we always learn really valuable lessons, now we can use those lessons. The most important and difficult things I have learned have come to me at the times when I screwed up the most. I don't regret anything in my life because my screw ups have taught me, helped me and made me successful.

If you were lost while out in your car would you drive around for the rest of your life without stopping and checking for directions or look at a map and change your route? Or would you really continue forever knowing deep down you were going the wrong way?

If you were a formula follower and are now reading this book, I am guessing you already had doubts that the formula wasn't all it was cracked up to be. Or maybe you are just curious as to what an alternative formula looks like. Well this is it, I don't think there can be a more alternative formula to the academic and career based one but I can say that it's a lot more fun and infinitely more rewarding.

My formula is not new or unique to me in any way. A lot of entrepreneurs rejected the academic and career route to pursue their dreams. I have compiled a small list here so you can see the diversity of successful people who rejected education and a formal route to an amazing career path.

Richard Branson - Left school at sixteen and started his first venture Student Magazine. Richard is known the world over for his great spirit of adventure inside and outside of business. I mostly admire him for his tenacity when taking on the established large companies and showing the world that anyone can achieve anything. His autobiography is a must read for anybody interested in free enterprise.

Michael Dell - Dropped out of college at nineteen and with just one thousand dollars started Dell Inc making PCs. Dell became one of the largest and most profitable PC manufactures in the world and still dominates the world computer hardware market to this day. Proving my point that you don't need a huge a mount of money to make more money.

Coco Channel - The perfume Channel No.5 has immortalised her name but Gabrielle Coco Channel was an orphan with little education. She was a seamstress who turned the fashion establishment upside down by using methods, styles and fabrics for women that were reserved only for men at the time. She was certainly a person who didn't care what people thought, we can all learn something from her.

Walt Disney - Dropped out of school at sixteen and went on to become the greatest and best known animator of all time. His achievements in film making and creating theme parks are well known and speak for themselves. Walt always laughed at his doubters and many said he was nuts. I love the way he proved them all wrong and today the Disney Corporation is worth billions.

Steve Jobs - Co founder of Apple and Pixar dropped out of college after just one semester; he worked at Atari before founding one of the most successful tech companies of all time Apple Computers. Now called just Apple Inc, Steve Jobs still oversees the development of great products like the iPod, iPhone and iPad. He is another outspoken person who does not care what others think, a very driven and determined man.

Henry Ford - Worked as a machinist after leaving school at sixteen. He later founded the Ford motor company and revolutionised car production, as well as many other mass produced items by refining the assembly line production method.

Bill Gates - Until recently the world's richest man, he skipped lessons to work on computers loaned to his school. Bill dropped out of Harvard to start the Microsoft corporation with his friend Paul Allen. I admire and relate to the way Bill "stretched the truth" a bit to secure their first contract by promising their program was ready when it wasn't but they worked on it day and night to deliver on time, the client was happy, they didn't know it wasn't ready before and the rest is history.

7. Am I arrogant?

A colleague once told me that others thought I was arrogant but he was pretty sure that I was just full of confidence. Once I got over the shock that other people were saying I was arrogant, I started to listen to what he said. At the time I was only about twenty years old and most of my peers in London working in the city were between twenty eight and thirty five, they had gone to university, worked in a couple of low level jobs and were now working their way up the ladder a bit. On the other hand I had bypassed all of that, found a niche in I.T. that was in demand at the time and was making bags of money.

After working for just one year at the private hospital I was lucky enough to be working on some new networking operating systems from Microsoft that were replacing the old mainframe and terminal based systems in large companies. Email and the Internet were just starting to take off as corporate tools and not just something geeky kids were messing about with in their bedrooms. The long and short of it was that my skills were in demand at that particular time and very soon I found myself earning great money.

I was surprised how colleagues were afraid to move jobs, actually scared to go somewhere else and earn twice the money. I didn't even want proper employment contracts at the places I worked, as I soon learned that billing by the hour as a contractor was far more lucrative.

I can tell you now if you have any fear or lack some basic confidence you will never get very far. Sometimes I wonder if I have a screw loose because I can be so cavalier about work, investments or any big commitments, but to achieve anything other than the ordinary then you quite literally have to hang it all out there.

This might sound daunting and you don't feel confident enough but don't worry, everyone can feel like that sometimes. If I am struggling with confidence or motivation on a project I let things build inside me for a while, I don't rush things if the fire doesn't come straight away. It can be particularly difficult if others around you are being negative about what you want to do but give yourself time to build your confidence and evaluate your plan. Stick to what you want, what you are passionate about, what you care about and you can overcome almost anything.

This is where ditching the negative people in your life can really benefit you. I will always rather be without family and friends if they are only going to fill my head with negativity. My core group of friends and family I now spend my time with are purely inspirational to me and hopefully I am inspirational to them too. I have had some criticism for this advice but my answer is always the same; if I get bogged down helping one person who will not be helped then many others will suffer by not getting my help. We should all be selective and economical with our efforts and the people we surround ourselves with. That way our lives are better and so are many more who we come into contact with. It sounds contradictory but it's true; the more selective you are, the more people you will help.

I must admit I enjoyed working at the hospital, I made some great friends and experienced a lot. When I was initially head hunted for another job I was reluctant to leave but I had a great Irish manager at the time who gave me some very decent advice, advice that I have shared with people ever since and it's this: If the company you work for could make more money (even just a small amount) or they could increase the company's value (even just a bit) by firing you, they would do it in a heartbeat without thinking about you twice. This is the true and realistic loyalty they would show to you, so repay them with the same loyalty; if you have an opportunity somewhere else that would benefit you more (even just a bit) or a chance of more money (even a small amount) then you should go for it.

I have never given much thought or care to even think about failure, when things didn't go to plan, I moved on, I did not feel embarrassment and I wasn't bothered by what others might say or think when something didn't work out. Let me tell you now you are never immune from failure or negative things happening. You will lose your job or a job won't work out for you, a house sale might fall through or something more serious like experiencing bankruptcy, these things happen every day to people. Who cares? Pick yourself up, dust yourself down and move on. The greatest boxers are not always the biggest hitters, in fact often they are not, the best fighters, the real enduring champions are the ones who can take the most punishment, pick themselves up and win in the end.

My friends and I joke now of the times when I contracted myself out to different companies and often if I didn't like the job or the person in charge, I would stay in the pub on a

Friday lunch time and send someone back to the office or phone from my mobile to let them know I wouldn't be coming back. I really was not bothered; if it was not good for me then I wasn't going to get out of bed (or the pub) for it. I would then make some calls to agents to find me something for Monday and enjoy my long weekend. I admit I had the advantage of being in demand but that time really taught me to recognise what was good for ME and I was learning to work a bit to earn some money to enjoy my life; I was working to live not living to work.

I must admit you do have to be thick skinned at times but from a young age I don't think I have been too bothered with what others think of me..........as long as I win in the end! If all this means I am arrogant then so be it, I would prefer to be this way, experience life, have no fear and win in the end rather than sit still and go nowhere.

8. Hard work and learning

Often people want something for nothing; they wait for something to land in their laps like a lottery win, some inheritance or a chance promotion. These people will moan if someone else achieves something through hard work, they will be jealous because they think that person was fortunate and something landed in their lap, they don't understand how to achieve anything. If by chance you are one of those people, please stop now and do the world a favour by making something happen for yourself, stop looking at others and concentrate on YOU!

There are also quite a few who only want the easy option, they don't want to do any hard thinking, put in any major effort or try too hard. Unfortunately I know a lot of people in this category and I know they will be reading this book and scanning for the "get rich quick, easy route to millions" sections so they can scam their way to riches. I believe this book contains the easiest route to wealth and freedom but this route also includes some hard work. You have to put some effort in I'm afraid, other than winning the lottery, you won't find a system to make a lot of money without some effort.

Two thousand five hundred years ago it was Confucius that first said something along the lines of "Find a job you love and you will never do a days work in your life", it was true then and it is still true now. There are some that are so lazy they can't even be bothered to do the things they enjoy, it's sad but true nonetheless. They are the kind to buy this book but not read it, they might scan it for some useful information but they won't take the time to read and digest it properly. Hopefully that is not you. I genuinely believe there are millions of "unlazy" people working in jobs they don't care for very much who given the right motivation and if they are doing what they love, will work harder, make a lot more money and be much happier in their lives.

I constantly remind myself to stick to what I enjoy and love so I don't get bored or fed up. I think this is why people often look at me and see me enjoying myself and having a great time and think I never work but they are wrong. I am on the go all the time, often putting in long days week in week out, travelling from place to place (for work not pleasure) and tiring myself out, but I love it! I also like to play hard, I will often work non stop for a number of months but then stop and enjoy myself for a month and search for new opportunities for fun and take in what's going on in the world.

About three years ago a junior member of staff at one of my consultancy customers spotted me getting out of my new car. He remarked on how nice it was and how wealthy I must be to own such a vehicle. I don't normally like very expensive cars because I usually scratch them, or someone else scratches it for me and I don't like the feeling when that happens so I often stick to a nice, reliable vehicle that I won't worry about if someone keys it. I also like the type of vehicle I can drive up to my vineyard without worrying about damaging. My current favourite vehicle is an old V8 pickup; it's like a well-worn jacket or pair of shoes that just feel comfortable. I'm getting to the point where I don't need status symbols in my life.

I do like cars though and occasionally I will spend out for something special. On this particular occasion it was probably one of the nicest cars I had had at that point. This young guy was probably about twenty three years old and he actually said the phrase "it's not fair" that I could afford to have an expensive car like that. I guess he meant it wasn't fair that I could afford it and he could not. I sat down with him and explained that fair had absolutely nothing to do with it and I had worked very hard to achieve my wealth. I had to bite my tongue because it was particularly difficult to take this from a young chap who was consistently late, the last member of staff to arrive and the first one to leave at the end of the day. Because this was a customer's employee, I had to be nice and explain politely what I wanted to say.

I spent quite some time explaining to that young man that at nineteen years of age, in my first job, I consistently worked twelve or more hours a day and when I say consistently, I mean pretty much every day. Then at the weekends I would come into the office when nobody was there and work on my own little projects, even just reading some of the books in the office so I could progress as quickly as possible. All of this was unpaid; I was only paid for thirty seven hours a week, that was it, no overtime, no additional time off, nothing at all was given to me for the massive amounts of overtime I put in. I didn't want anything either, I was happy to be learning so much and knew that this would help me achieve something.

Some of my friends from school had been lucky enough to go to university and at that time, from nineteen to twenty years of age, I told myself repeatedly that this was my only chance to get somewhere, I couldn't go to university but I had this shot and I could not blow it.

As I mentioned before I was not a big computer enthusiast and I did not really enjoy the work I just knew it would help me get somewhere, so I got on with it. I used my initiative at the hospital in my first job and took old computers out of the store room, built half decent working machines from the parts and set up small test networks in the corner of the computer room. I would work on the old computers any chance I could get and that included at night and at weekends. I wasn't particularly geeky, I didn't do it for fun, I just wanted to learn and get on. I knew it would get me somewhere.

So when I finished describing all this to the young guy who thought it wasn't fair I had a nice car, I then explained that I was talking about one year that happened eleven years ago and since then I had worked just as hard but also took more risks. I now asked "so now, what do you think is not fair about it?" He didn't have an answer but I hoped he might take something from what I said and use it but to my astonishment, his behaviour did not change at all. This guy was already tipped for promotion by the senior management IF he could show a bit more commitment, information which I shared with him to encourage him. He was still often late or arrived bang on time, he usually left exactly on time too, but on the odd occasion when he really had to work late, he made such a song and dance about it, you would think he had worked late every day for a year.

This episode made me realise that there are some people who need more help than just a short conversation and even some that will never be helped; they moan about their situation and how others have it better but they are totally unwilling to do anything about it. Don't be one of them, you are in charge of your life and only you can do something about it.

During the first year at the hospital I would have quite literally slept there if I could have. I loved being on such a steep learning curve and I wanted more, I couldn't get enough of the knowledge and experience I was getting. Whilst writing this and thinking of the young people I have worked with and seen working at different places, I don't think I have seen that level of commitment in many people since. It is only while writing this book I have heard from a few youngsters who are making a massive effort to find a different path. Perhaps it was the fact I felt I had nowhere to go back to and that failure really was not an option for me because I could not go back to the hostel. If that is the case then it's not difficult for people to have the same attitude; don't look back too much and keep moving forward with ambition and enthusiasm. That's all I had and to be honest there have been many times since when that is all I had but it was all I needed to achieve an invaluable amount of freedom and a better life than I could have dreamed of.

9. Being Critical

I am so critical of myself, it's crazy and I have always been that way. I studied photography for a while and I created some great artwork that I should have been proud of but I was sometimes too critical of it, constantly looking for the kind of perfection that is hard to find. I am not talking about self deprecation or beating myself up, I have plenty of confidence in my own abilities, I am talking about constructive criticism and recognising strengths and weaknesses.

I have started to realise that not everyone is like this and in fact it could be quite a rare trait. I see most people making similar mistakes over and over again. Not the same mistakes because that would be plain stupid, but similar mistakes. They will go from one bad job to another, making consistently bad financial decisions, they take awful, impulsive decisions without thinking ahead properly, with no idea about the long term consequences of their actions, being lazy but kidding themselves and everyone else that they are trying hard.

I never really thought about it too deeply before, but over the last six months I have been surrounded by quite a few people doing this and I have analysed some others that I have known well for some time that fall into this category. What I have found is that they are very defensive if anyone offers advice, or heaven forbid, if anyone makes an outright criticism of a decision they made or something they did, even if it is quite obviously true. To clarify; in most of these cases it has not been me offering the advice, I have just been observing.

People just do not want to admit their faults or mistakes and even when they do, they will not analyse where they went wrong and why, they just briefly admit something under protest and then try to forget about it. By doing this they do not recognise or understand the underlying issues and reasons for their errors, so they continue to make similar mistakes again and again.

I will let you in on a little secret: It's all your fault! The way your life has turned out: Your fault, it's your life, if you don't like it do something about it! The reason people treat you badly: Your fault, you let them! No money? Your fault, you are in charge of your destiny, if you want more money, go and get some. Don't come back to me with excuses like: health problems, bad parents, wrong neighbourhood, no education etc. etc. because it doesn't cut any ice with me. I have had serious health problems, I was on the streets as a teenager, I don't have any real qualifications and I suffer from dyslexia. Guess what? Nobody gives a crap! Everyone has issues to deal with so get over yourself.

I fully expect a good portion of the people reading this book to have stopped by now because they will never admit what I am saying is true and they are not intelligent enough to become a better, wealthier person. If you are one of the few still reading this you are at least half way there.

When you achieve your goals you will see, (and you may already see) there will always be those that want to believe their own specific situation, or external forces, have affected why they have not achieved anything and held them back. They will say we were purely fortuitous and subconsciously they will hate us for rubbing their noses in their own laziness and lack of achievement. What they will never understand is that I don't want to rub anyone's nose in it or show off. All I want to do is help people see things the way I do, so that hopefully many more people can see all the opportunities open to them, enabling them to achieve their dreams, whatever they might be.

10. Recognising and Creating Opportunities

Information is power. Read and watch the news and not just one newspaper or news channel, check out all of them, even the ones you don't like, local, national and international, trade press, magazines, everything you have time to digest. This is how big bank investors, stock and commodity traders and foreign exchange dealers work the markets; they absorb and use vast amounts of information about what is going on in the world.

One of the best and worst sources information is other people. Get out and meet as many people as you can, they will keep you informed and everyone you meet is a potentially useful future contact. You do have to get used to sifting through what people tell you and recognise reality from rumour, but in my opinion there is no better way of finding useful information and getting contacts at the same time. Networking clubs (the right ones), local bars and pubs, coffee shops, business clubs and sports clubs, (big and small) are all great places to make contacts and get regular info. Note; you must go regularly to build up relationships to get the best out of it.

Everyone you meet holds loads of potential opportunities for you. The more you speak to them, the more chance you have of hearing about those opportunities and the more people you have in your network, the further the net is spread. People truly do buy from people. Business people and entrepreneurs don't make their money by hiding in an office or standing over their workforce watching their every move. They get out in the world and talk to as many people as possible to get new ideas and make things happen.

Everywhere I go I observe everything. My wife sometimes calls me "The Terminator" because I see/scan everything and I retain nearly everything. This is not a special trick or talent, anyone can do it. I am literally looking for opportunities. Land for sale, houses for sale, what new businesses I haven't seen before, can that idea be copied or improved? What don't they have here that I have seen somewhere else? What do certain things cost in this area compared to somewhere else and why?

I do the same with conversations and meetings; I am scanning what they say to pick out what could be useful. What useful contact did they mention that saved them money on that deal? What loophole did she use to save some tax and can I do that? What is everyone saying they need but can't find, is there a business in that? With all these observations you might only use 5% of the best ideas but you have to try and take them all in to find the 5% worth anything.

Two things I want to add here: don't steal any ideas from people and if you are totally ruthless and mercenary you will be found out. You do need solid people, friends, contacts et al around you and nobody will help you twice if you use people too much.

11. Examples of Opportunities I Saw and Took

I have purposely left out too much of my business dealings from this book because this is not a boring corporate text book. However, because I wanted to include some examples of the opportunities and luck I created for myself; here are some recent fun/side investments I made, so you can get an idea of what I am doing on a daily basis.

Property in the UK

Bricks and mortar on freehold land in the right circumstances can be one of the best and safest investments we can make. There are a lot of pitfalls however. Finding the right deals, getting things done myself and developing things personally have helped me make a few good bets on property over the years. There is more detail on these property investments further on in this chapter.

The boat

An acquaintance of mine, that later became a good friend, owned a boat on the Thames in Oxford near where I lived. I didn't know him too well at the time although I visited his boat and enjoyed it, but mostly I liked what he told me; it's a very cheap place to stay in Oxford, free parking in the city (which is worth it's weight in gold alone) and the boats hold their value.

I was interested so I asked A LOT of questions. What transpired was his boat was specialist and expensive, too expensive for me but in the next marina there were more modern boats that were cheaper and ones that needed fixing up, going for next to nothing. I was bold, asked for some help making contact with the owner of the other marina and got a name and phone number.

I went to visit the other marina and had a look at some of the boats for sale but I didn't like any of them and they were still a bit pricey. I did see one I liked the look of that obviously needed some work, but looked impressive. It was stood out of the water on some barrels and did look a bit sorry for itself, but was obviously once a great looking vessel. I immediately piped up "what about that one?" I was told it wasn't for sale but the guy that owned it hadn't visited for a long time and owed the marina money so they would like it if it was for sale. I said "fine, call the owner and tell them I'll offer him 3000 for it" (more than half what the other shabby ones were selling for). "I will but I don't think he will take it, it's worth a lot more and worth at least 10000 in a half reasonable state" the marina owner told me. I replied "Well I can really only afford 3000 so offer him that and see what he says". I think the owner of the boat owed quite a bit to the marina so he was happy to take the money and pay off his debt.

I could have not bothered to ask all the questions from my acquaintance in the first place because he didn't readily offer the information and I might not want to appear rude by pressing for all the details. I could have just accepted his was a specialist boat and assumed they probably all cost that much. I could have just accepted that these boats were the ones for sale, decided I didn't like them and go home. I could have offered a higher price because that's what the marina owner was angling at. I could also have thought I don't know anything about boats. But no, I made it happen and after some work and talking to other boat owners at the marina, my wife and I got our lovely boat ship shape, insured, in the water and useful. Now the boat is worth 10000 from an investment of about 4500 and about two weeks work. I am not going to retire on that but it's better than any boring savings account and it's as good as money in the bank.

Foreign land

My wife is originally from Hungary and after visiting many times we decided it would be nice to have a property in Hungary near the lake Balaton, which is a fantastic place, not that well known, but a popular destination for Hungarians, Germans and Dutch tourists. It is beautiful in the summer, with fantastic weather and very long summers. There are lots of local vineyards so there's also lots of great wine in the area.

We quickly realised that any houses near the lake would cost more than we could invest in a second home so, me being me, investigated and asked lots and lots of questions. What I found out was that many small vineyards had press houses and wine cellars that Hungarians also used as small holiday homes. Even though they were technically agricultural buildings, people converted parts of the building into living accommodation and this was accepted.

At that time agricultural land and buildings could only be sold to Hungarians and this had kept prices very low. So as my wife is Hungarian we were able to buy a huge piece of land with a press house and wine cellar on a hill with the most breath taking view over the lake. We are now in the process of building a house on the land and we have bought a neighbouring lot even cheaper than the first. I have a feeling that these two investments together will turn out to be the greatest investments of my life. I don't know the figures because I don't want to know, I want to keep this property as a place for my children to grow up. However I do know this IS the kind of investment I could retire on.

To be perfectly honest my wife deserves much of the credit on this one because at one point I was ready to give up the search. After finding out a lot of information on vineyards and press houses, we searched and searched for the right one in the right location but we just could not find the right one. I was starting to resign myself to the fact we probably would not find one and we should put the idea on hold for a while. My wife had other ideas, she knew how much it meant to me and she really wanted to find the right place. Her perseverance night after night of searching online ads finally paid off. She eventually found an ad for a press house and vineyard with a view of the lake and a price only slightly over budget. We almost didn't call though because the total area size described seemed a little small, especially for the asking price. We did call though and found out there had been a misprint and they missed a 0 off the total area so it was ten times bigger than what we were expecting! When we went to see it we were bowled over with the size and view, we knew straight away it was the place we wanted.

A bit of detail on these investments

I don't want to bore you to death with every good decision I made or every avenue I explored but decided against going down (especially on the business side). However I do want to go into two property investments in a bit more detail to give you some insight into how they came about.

Detail 1

I want to go into more detail on this foreign investment property. On the face of it, it seems like a nice, easy, cheap, high return investment but behind the scenes it took a long time to come together for various reasons and was so difficult at times, I think a lot of people would have given up if they had not kept their eye on the end game and stayed focused on what a great investment it is. Therein lies another tip; keep your eyes on the prize. I often tell myself if it was easy everyone would be doing it and if it's still for sale at a cheap price, it's probably because there is a problem.

Most people walk away at the first sign of trouble but I am a stubborn bastard and if I can see there is a good investment to be had cheap, because everyone else has been scared off, then I will find out what it will take in time, effort and cash to overcome the problem. Quite often it's just hassle that people are avoiding, not money, so if you have time and patience you can get the best bargains.

Firstly my wife and I spent weeks trawling through property details, making phone calls and visiting property after property that were just over priced and disappointing. This process was slightly more difficult to manage than usual at the time due to our commitments in the UK and the area we were looking in was around the lake Balaton in Hungary. Eventually we found what seemed like THE place but on paper it seemed too good to be true, especially as it was half the price of all the other garbage we had looked at, but when we saw it and the view over the lake we knew it was the place. However we also saw why it was cheap:

The property investment I am talking about had three apparent problems:

1. The advert for the property had been misprinted and stated an incorrect amount of land for sale.

2. The presale and legal process was difficult because the communication was tough for many reasons, perhaps partly our fault, but I felt the seller was difficult to deal with. Also because the property was split into two title numbers, legally owned by three different people, the seller needed a quick sale due to personal problems and needed the cash, literally had to have it in cash.

3. Although the property was in a prime location, near a tourist resort, with a great view and close enough to the motorway, the access to the property was awful, across a very long and rutted track.

Problem number 3 was actually something which resolved itself by chance quite quickly; we spoke to someone locally who mentioned a new road was being built near to where the property is. When we looked into it further we discovered the new road would create a new and easier access. Work for the road was scheduled to start within a year. That was one issue dealt with and once again it showed that on the face of it things looked a bit crap, but after some research and digging around solutions often present themselves.

The other two reasons don't seem to be much when summarised and stated here, but they constituted months of headaches, many difficult phone calls, missed phone calls, arguments, legal wrangling and a small amount of ranting and shouting from more than one person. As it dragged on I did say once that I just didn't want to go on with it anymore and I would look for another investment property to spend my money on but after a nights sleep I persevered. Actually looking back I think I reconsidered more than once.

I can't stress to you enough how glad I am we pressed on when others would have given up. The property is the place I now call "The Ranch", we paid a tiny fraction of it's value. We have added to it by buying the neighbouring land and property too, we are in the process of securing planning permission and developing the building already there. I doubt I will ever want to sell it but what a great piece of equity that I can use to borrow against to invest elsewhere.

My point with this example is that where others would have walked away either at the start due to the bad access, complicated issues and errors surrounding the sale or during the middle of the deal when it was dragging on and causing headaches, we stood firm and got a bargain. The reason we got a bargain was because we were prepared to go where nobody else would and stay until the job was done.

Detail 2

The property investments in Oxfordshire started when I had been developing a property in a really pleasant village whilst living in it. I had made quite a bit of profit but the property didn't have much more potential left after I had worked on it, so I decided it would be good to put my money into another property that I could maximise the profit from. I had also been in the house for four years and I was getting itchy feet anyway.

What I wanted was a house that needed work and could maybe be extended or added to in some way. What I really wanted was a bigger, detached property in a village or on the outskirts of a village with a huge garden, but these were becoming rarer in Oxfordshire due to developers building more houses in large gardens of houses they had bought and the ones left were commanding very high prices. Undeterred I decided to search anyway and see what I could find. After visiting a lot of estate agents and driving around looking for SALE boards, I realised that agents were only giving out details of houses they wanted to sell. I know that might sound strangely obvious but they were pushing certain properties and were reluctant to give me details of others I had seen, probably because they were cheaper. I'm not sure of all the reasons why they do this but it became clear I could not rely on agents to give me all the information I needed, so I turned to the internet.

I knew I couldn't drive up and down every street in the whole county looking for properties for sale, so I used two good websites for searching for property for sale, using the broadest searches possible and sifting through hundreds of details manually. Now maybe I just have an eye for detail or, like my wife says, maybe I do scan the world like the terminator but I noticed on my web searches that if I narrowed down my search criteria, the same houses the agents were pushing would show up. I don't think many other people would have noticed this, they would have gone on the web done some very specific searches, printed out the details, gone to few agents got a few more details and they would have trusted what they were given.

I question everything, so I opened up my search criteria and did a search on detached properties in the whole county AND ten miles around the outskirts as well. I also opened up the search criteria of my price range, I put the starting price at zero as I realised some properties were listed without a price, so would only show up as zero asking price and I pushed up my upper limit knowing I could probably beat down the price to what I could afford.

Oxfordshire and the surrounding area is an area of well over one thousand square miles and my open search criteria brought up a lot of search results. In fact I sifted through close to three thousand property details. It was quite a boring and at times disheartening job, but just the fact I was seeing so many good properties that had not been brought to my attention before spurred me on to find the bargain that had been hiding from me. I know many people would not bother with this much diligence and boring searching but what if I told you it was worth in the region of £80,000 of saving on the property I eventually found and a house of the size and type, with development potential, I would never have found otherwise? Would you spend a week doing searches and sifting through thousands of property details then?

Research shows people watch, on average, four hours of TV a day. If you add to that time spent on video games and other mindless activities, you can see that you can easily find the time to sift through information to find yourself an investment worth tens of thousands in profit. Can't you? It's worth noting that I employ this method for all my investment scanning and searching now whether it be property related or not. I cast the net wide and I sift through as much information as possible, even looking outside the area I was originally looking just to check all the options. I never trust what someone tells me I will check for myself and still question it before making a decision. It might seem cynical but it works.

The house was slightly outside the fashionable areas of Oxfordshire (but still in the county), I liked that because it was unspoiled and the locals were genuine, nice people, not toffee nosed townies having a jaunt in the countryside. After buying the property I got planning permission to turn it from a relatively modest four bedroom house into a six bedroom grand home. The garden was huge and backed onto open countryside, the local shop and pub were friendly and welcoming. As it happens the property market dived after I bought it but the planning permission I secured on it stopped it losing any value when all other properties were losing value on a daily basis and it was still a property of the size and type that would have been out of my league at that time, had I not spent so much time and effort finding it.

I should mention how I got the planning permission, as some of you living in that area will know how hard it can be and this is another great example of recognising opportunities and good contacts. Spotting and using good contacts is a skill worth developing and it is often true what they say "It's not what you know it's who you know". Many people will use that as an excuse moaning they don't know the right people and that's why they can't get anywhere. I have found that getting out there and meeting those influential people is easier than you might think and they are often quite friendly, after all they are just people like you and I.

I had done some freelance IT work for an architect and planning consultant for many years and after probing a bit, asking questions and being generally interested about his work when I was at his office we became acquaintances and shared information. I helped him out a few times for free with some computer issues he had on the understanding that he could help me if required in the future. Here is a great tip, be friendly, ask questions and be interested in everyone you meet and meet as many people as you can. Some people will not be interested and won't be good contacts, but others will. You can help them if they need help and you never know when pulling in that favour will be useful. Everyone knows that the best advertising and marketing is word of mouth; the more people you meet and who like you equals more people you have out there saying great things about you and what you do.

So I had a great architect and planning consultant to pull a few favours in from, my next hurdle was the local council who would ultimately make the planning decision.

When I first moved to the village I went to the local pub a few times and realised it was the place where most of the local business was discussed and thrashed out. After a few months of moving in to the village, on one of my visits to the pub, I heard they were struggling to fill a place on the parish council. I was told that the village was in danger of losing the parish council to a nearby town which would be awful for the village. I needed some inside knowledge on what was required to get planning permission locally so I jumped at it.

I had not told anyone of my ideas for developing the property yet and I knew a position on the parish council (although it shouldn't) would give me a better chance of a planning decision going my way, if only because I would get to know what the requirements were for planning in the area. Maybe others would not make that connection or think they don't know how to be a parish councillor, or perhaps some would think it's a lot of effort and extra time so they can't be bothered. However, once again, is it worth a few hours a week when it could be worth tens of thousands to you? I didn't know anything about being a parish councillor but who cares? I knew enough to know it would give me a head start with my planning permission and that's all I needed to know, I didn't care if it needed a few hours a week. If you don't go to your mundane job every day, a few hours helping some friends in return for a few favours, a few hours at the pub and on the parish council to make a hundred grand in six months is worth it, right? Especially now you have plenty more time to do other things to make even more money in that six months as well.

I can't stress enough how important it is to get out and be friendly, find out what's going on and make good contacts locally and everywhere you go. It takes perseverance sometimes, people won't always automatically warm to you but put yourself out there and it will pay dividends, not just financially but personally and emotionally too. It gives me a good feeling to meet new people I like and especially if I can help them in some way, not everything comes back to me but I believe in some kind of Karma. In some way I am sure the more you give to the world in time and energy the more you will get back. Don't let people take advantage of you though, remember who you work for, you.

One last thing I want to say on these investments of mine is that they were opportunities that I looked for and found, they were personal to me, opened up for me and in some cases were only available to me. Your opportunities will be different, your contacts will be different, your circumstances will be different but your opportunities are just as good, unique and maybe even better than mine.

12. Vision

Being able to see through a dirty, run down house and envision a renovated, beautiful home is a very useful talent good property developers have. It is a talent that can be learned and is important for all entrepreneurs.

Having the vision to see something where nothing exists now is a great quality that anyone can do. It's really easy and it works like this: Are you that wealthy that you can afford every nice thing you clap eyes on? OK if not, then you can still have what you want if you can work on it. The finished product is expensive and has a premium attached because someone else has had the hassle of "finishing" and "polishing" the product. If you can recognise the potential in something before it is finished and polished and you can create the finished article yourself, then you will have yourself a bargain or the perfect investment to sell for a profit.

Look at some houses or buildings and start thinking how you could make the most of it in the area it stands in, on the street it's on and how profitable it could be. I do this with nearly everything I look at, buildings, vehicles, businesses, land, even people. It might sound odd to say people, but most people are not only your friends and they see you as a potential contact to make something out of or they find you useful in some way, so make the most of them too. I can count my real friends on one hand and there is research to suggest it is hard to maintain real and meaningful relationships (outside of your family) with more than five people at a time. As I have mentioned already in this book; make your relationships and contacts count.

Having foresight and vision is important in many ways, not just for spotting a bargain or potential investment, it can save you from making a lot of mistakes and save you time and money too. Being able to analyse a situation and formulate a plan in my head is something I have learned over time and it's quite easy to do. The one thing I stick to is: don't get emotional. Once I have made a crazy and seemingly irrational decision to invest where nobody else is, I try to make that the last bit of decision-making my heart or gut makes in the process. After that point I try to remember to make logical, considered choices and never make an emotional response to problems or situations.

This brings me on to a related subject and one which I have had a hard time explaining in the past. It is a type of vision that is required to break away from a static life.

I always say that people are too hung up on amounts of money like how much they earn, how much they have saved, how much cash they have on them right now, how much is my house worth or how much their car cost. I have always been different, I have always worked towards a better lifestyle. When I was in the homeless hostel I just wanted a better life; amounts of money and zeros on a bank balance were irrelevant. Ever since then I have deviated at times but generally speaking I have been working towards a nicer lifestyle.

There are a few penthouse apartments in New York and London worth more than my vineyard and property looking over the lake and maybe even more than all my other assets put together, but I wouldn't trade my life for a life in a city apartment. I made a decision a long time ago that I wanted a piece of beautiful land, some horses, freedom, space and fresh air for me and my family to enjoy. I also wanted more time and energy to enjoy the outdoor life and travel. It became obvious that where I was in the world and what I was doing at that time was restricting me completely from fulfilling those ambitions, so I found the place and life where I could afford, develop and enjoy all those things I wanted. Out of that has come numerous other opportunities and good luck that have improved my life even more.

This is no different from when I lived in the homeless hostel and wanted a better life for myself; I saw better and easier opportunities to get the life I wanted elsewhere, so I went and took those opportunities. I didn't get bogged down with how much it would cost or staying where I was for any sentimental reasons. I went wherever I needed to go, did what I had to do and that gave me all the things I wanted and much, much more.

I see people constantly chasing amounts of money thinking it will bring them the things they want but inevitably it does not. Ultimately a lot of people believe money can buy us freedom but we already have freedom, in many respects money takes away our freedom. We need to concentrate on the actual THINGS we want in life and they are out there for us, we just need to go and get them.

13. Generating and Developing Ideas and Luck

Understand that opportunities develop in stages, with involvement from many different people with changes, improvements and adaptations along the way. Nobody wakes up one day with a super idea that they immediately implement into a multi-million, international success story within 24 hours. Good ideas have a life of there own but you have to allow them to develop, if you don't you will kill it all by yourself. It has happened so many times that someone single mindedly pursues an idea, or often an invention that they refuse to adapt or let anyone else be involved with and that potentially wealth making idea or invention is eventually killed by the very person who created it, before it makes any money and usually at a point when it has probably lost a lot of money unnecessarily.

Any idiot can have a great idea, ideas are everywhere, ideas are easy but implementation and execution of good ideas is as rare as rocking horse crap. That is because most people have had an idea and then said "someone should do that!" Why should someone else do that, why can't YOU do that? That's when the excuses would come; I don't have the start up capital, I don't have the right contacts and so on. Before dismissing the idea: do you know the ACTUAL start up cost amount and could it be reduced slightly to an amount you could find or borrow (not just the bank but friends and relatives)? What contacts do you need exactly and why can't you go out and find the right contacts?

As some opportunities can stall for a while I have never been afraid to have five or six ideas, investments or opportunities running simultaneously. I personally don't like juggling more than five or six and realistically it is usually no more than three because I don't feel that I can give each project the attention, learning, dealing and enthusiasm they need, but I know others that juggle a lot more. If you have a husband, wife, partner, boyfriend or girlfriend that wants to help then that obviously makes it easier to cope with more.

As you are waiting on progress with one project you can concentrate on another for a while. I believe the reason a lot of people lose interest, or start thinking a project is not working in the early stages is because it does take time. Projects do get held up and sometimes projects almost seem to pause for indeterminate amounts of time. This does not mean they are dead, just on hold, waiting. Waiting for another contact to give some input, waiting for the right information or investment to get going again. This is the point most people give up, don't. Put it on the back burner, keeping your ear to the ground and eyes open for the thing it needs to get going again, at the same time start running with that other idea/opportunity. I used to get carried away with this and have too many irons in the fire, so I would recommend staying focused and passionate about a set number of projects, don't spread yourself too thin but have enough to keep you interested and, importantly, the income flowing in.

Self-sufficient, single minded wheeler dealers without proper employment have often been portrayed in the media as comical, stupid people or lazy bums but the world is full of very successful people that do not have a "proper job" or their business is not a huge venture employing loads of people. There are freelancers, self employed sales people, small business owners, consultants and different kinds of investors that earn many times the average salary and enjoying life more than they would in a "proper job".

Have you ever taken a day off work and driven around at 11am on a weekday thinking: How come there is so much traffic and what do all these people do? Not all of them but a good portion of them are people like me that don't want a nine to five job with a difficult boss and annoying colleagues, we want to be in control and we are doing well. With some nerve, a bit of hard work and the ability to spot opportunities learned from this book, you or anyone can join us.

Get out, get out, get out! I have learned only recently that my most prosperous periods occur at the time when I get out the most. I have also seen people that run businesses or are self employed that don't get out much who are always moaning that things are not happening for them. This is because by getting out you meet new people, these new contacts might not all be useful but you often only need just one to turn around the fortunes of a project you are working on. I have met great friends, contacts and business associates in the pub, local council and residents meetings. I have even just talked to people in the street because they were speaking English in a foreign country, so I introduced myself and ended up helping them with a business venture.

Getting out and about also gives you opportunities to see new things, new shops and businesses that could give you ideas, new ways of doing things that might inspire a new project, even something as simple as a new billboard which is advertising something in a new way that helps you to advertise your product in a better way. You won't see these things or meet these people sat in an office, a workshop or at home.

Go and drive round for a few hours in some interesting place you don't know or usually go to, take a notepad and pen with you and write some notes on ideas you have. I guarantee once you start you won't be able to stop. I have the most prolific ideas and the best quality ideas when I go away on holiday and there are two reasons for this: because I am relaxed with no distractions but importantly I am seeing and hearing new things that I don't normally find out about in my bubble at home. Force yourself to get out, see new things and meet new people.

Here are some potential ideas for you to ponder:

- Freelance work

Many people make great money in the chosen field by quitting their day job and working freelance for different companies. It's possible to make more money with a lot more freedom and flexibility. This is how I started out on the road to financial independence.

- Property

It is one of the best known and easily accessible investment methods. Done right, making sure the investment has enough potential in the right area at the right time and property investments can be very lucrative.

- Investing in any good ideas

You may have noticed in the back of some newspapers small ads asking if you have an invention or idea worth investing in. The people taking out these ads sort through all the ideas that come through and select the best ones to invest in. You can do this with a relatively small amount of money, it just takes time to gather and sift through all the information that will come your way. This is a more direct and concentrated way of how most investors work.

- Alternative "Work from Home" options

99% of "Work from Home" options are scams to part people with their money or time with very little in return, however there are a few genuine potential "work from home" possibilities. Freelance work mentioned above is one of them.

Online tutoring in your field of expertise or hobby is another that can be done by creating course material and doing one to one sessions via web chat, Skype, Windows Live messenger or similar webcam video conferencing. Look up REAL work from home opportunities on the web, do loads of research, don't look for the easiest option and you might be surprised with the ideas you get.

- Write a book

Although it is a lot harder than I first thought I can recommend it as a very rewarding and worthwhile project.

- Make Something

Use your existing skills or hobby to make things. Hand made, quality products are in short supply in this day of mass produced items from the far east and consumers pay a premium for the good quality, locally made items you can produce.

- Do what you are good at

Most importantly, whatever you do, use the skills that you are best at and enjoy doing.

You might think these suggested ideas or your ideas and opportunities seem small but all big things start from small ideas.

Remember I mentioned Michael Dell started out with just $1000, started making PCs at home and now Dell Inc is a billion dollar industry.

To make a million you need to start by making a few hundred. The principles are the same and you have to start somewhere. If an idea is good it will evolve and grow all on its own, if you let it. Start small, think big.

14. Wasted Talent

The worst thing in the world is wasted talent. My wife says I can be geeky but a rare geek who can turn my geekiness into money. I'm a little embarrassed by that statement and I want to deny it but I get the essence of it. It is true there are a lot of "geeks" in their field of expertise or in their hobby who do nothing with their talents and knowledge. Is it bravery, guts or desperation (or all three) that encourages certain people to risk it all out there? I don't know for everyone else but more people should do it. Remember the Confucius quote I mentioned earlier? "If you do what you love for a living you will never do a day's work in your life." This world could do with all the raw talent it can get.

Committing to change and embracing a new life when I was living in the hostel was not that difficult, I really had nothing to lose and everything to gain but I understand it's not always that easy to commit to a massive change in your life. I have held back when I perceived I had more to lose. I once spent six months in a job I hated, being upset for believing the hype about the job that the boss gave me when I first took the job but the reality of the position was very different. It took me far too long to quit and do something else. I recently did a long contract for a company that treated employees badly, contractors badly and nearly everyone that had anything to do with them had nothing good to say about the company. It was depressing and I should have found something better sooner. In all the scenarios when I should have got out sooner there are others, the majority in fact who are still there in awful jobs, very unhappy, years later. I hope some of you are reading this and take a chance to do something different, something better. Life is too short not to isn't it?

Be who you want to be

This is an exercise I try and do regularly:

Look at all the periods of your life, look back and see when you were the funniest, happiest, most enjoyable person to be around. You are still that person, just let yourself be that person again and not just some of the time but all of the time. You will be the best person you can be when you are like that and you will be great for everyone around you. Inspire others, be a fun, confident and interesting person to spend time with.

Something to consider if you have children or you are thinking about having children is this:

Children don't always respond well to commands and heavy handed rules, they will often rebel against them without even knowing why. The best thing you can do when bringing up your children is set a great example. Be their role model; if you are happy, earn respect from people, work hard for what you want and if you are a great person to be around they will look up to you and they will want to be like you. If you are a good person and do all the things described here in this book and your children turn out just like you then there is nothing more you can ask for. We should want our children to surpass us, what better springboard to do this than to be just like us at our best, surely that's the optimum place for them to start?

Even adult friends and family are like this; what is the only thing that everyone gives but nobody takes? ADVICE. If you try and lecture, advise and wax lyrical to people about the contents of this book or your own successes after you start achieving your goals, do you think many people will really listen to you if they haven't made up their own mind about what you have to say? No, they won't, it's a sad fact but it's true, believe me I have tried. It is one of the reasons I decided to write this book because I wanted to reach some people that actually wanted to listen and learn something.

The next time you have a coffee or go to a dinner party with some friends (in fact most social group situations) take note that most people (not all) are not really listening to what is being said when other people are talking, they are just waiting for their turn to speak. This is not true of all people, all the time, but when you look out for it you will be surprised how often it happens.

Set a good example to people, be inspiring and people will follow, you don't need to shout about it, people will notice. If someone wants your advice they will ask for it and when they do they will actually listen to what you say. If someone chooses to buy this book they will read it and take from it what they wish but if you just give someone a few sound bites from it that mean something to you, that doesn't necessarily follow that it will mean anything to that particular person. If you recommend the book or give them a copy and they choose to read it, they will get far more from it.

At one particular place I worked, one member of the senior management team was the epitome of someone who never listened and only waited for his turn to talk, he dismissed anyone else's opinion without even taking it into consideration for a second; it couldn't possibly be a good idea because he didn't think of it. It wasn't just his staff that he treated in this way, I was also on the senior management team and we were all treated with the same contempt. He was arrogant to the extreme, incompetent in management and ridiculed by everyone behind his back for his shortcomings.

This is an extreme case but his persona sums up some unpleasant human characteristics that we all have at times. As well as not giving out unwelcome advice, try to listen more when people talk to you, consider other people's suggestions that you wouldn't have thought twice about before. We don't have to act on everything we hear but it really can broaden your thinking and increase your chances of success. As I pointed out earlier in the book, information is the key and other people are the best sources of that information but you won't learn anything if you are only waiting for your turn to talk. Learn to listen.

15. Keep Trying

I have had some pretty sizable set backs over the last fifteen years, I've been through a nasty illness that put me in hospital and gave me a pretty big scare, as well as sending one of my businesses under because I wasn't around enough to steer it through a rough patch while I was ill. Not too long after that I went through a divorce which was quite tough but worked out for the best in the end.

I am sure that I will be reading this book myself in years from now because I will be on a new life changing experience or suffering a little setback and I will need some motivation and inspiration. Our goals will change, our lives will move on and I am not so arrogant as to realise that I am still young, I have a lot of life ahead of me and I may find myself in a rut again sometime in the future.

The key is to start again with new goals and objectives mixed in with some old ones, but most importantly I know that with the right attitude and keeping an eye open for those opportunities, life will be fine. Usually we will be starting from a point much further ahead than we were last time. If only just further ahead with life skills, experience and knowing more of what we want and what we don't want.

When I made my first life change at nineteen years old in the hostel it was actually the second time I had ended up there. I never once thought that I hadn't moved forward and that my life couldn't get better. If anything, the fact I was there a second time probably pushed me into making my life changing decisions and motivated me more. If you don't succeed at something or you feel like things are not moving forward as you would like them just change your goals slightly, look at the bigger picture and move on. Don't get demotivated by small or even big set backs, learn from it, adapt and find a solution.

When you are confident and enthusiastic those opportunities will find you and more importantly you will find them. Now I have a huge amount of confidence in my belief that everything will always be OK, because no matter what has come up in my life when I was down and depressed nothing happened, but when I set my mind to it and I am willing to make something happen THEN the chances, luck and solutions have landed right in front of me. The same is true for anyone you just need to make sure you know how to spot those opportunities and use them.

16. Education

Without any formal education I would never be writing this book. I am grateful for an enormous amount that I learnt in school and I am very lucky to have been born and brought up in a country where a half decent education is provided free by the state (despite what people may think about the education system). The problem is I had learnt everything I needed to know and everything I use to this day by the time I was fourteen years old. Almost everything else I was exposed to in formal education after that point was largely a waste of time.

Despite what I previously stated in the chapter "Formula Followers" I have a lot of respect for academics and there are some merits to gaining qualifications, especially for doctors, lawyers and engineers etc. For the rest of us though we should recognise that after a certain point in schooling, the education system is run by academics for academics. Teachers, lecturers, head teachers, principals, all these people in most cases have never worked in the "real world". They do not know what is required of people in a commercial environment. I was told many times that if I did not go to university the only job opportunities open to me would be sweeping streets or digging holes. I am not the only one, I have heard many people of different ages from different schools and even different countries tell me that the same things were told to them. This was not something they said to me just to encourage me to go to university, those teachers believed it, you could tell by the conviction with which they told me and how often they said it.

My experience of working for some of the best companies in the world and the people I worked with there is that what those teachers told me was so far from the truth. Lots of great people I worked with in very well paid and important jobs had no university education and often had no formal qualifications for the job they were in. We got to where we were by being very good at what we did, by having the right attitude to the work and enjoying our jobs. Most teachers would not know this because they have not had a career in a commercial environment and had the pleasure of meeting all these people that do not have a university education, but still have great, rewarding, well paid and important careers.

I wonder how many people are out there that stack shelves in supermarkets or sweep streets instead of being the captains of industry that they are capable of being, because they believed their teachers when they told them that was the best life was going to offer if you didn't have a university education? So many young people with so much potential are literally written off by society and the education system every day. What would have happened if I had listened to them and not questioned what they said? Considering what I went through in my life immediately after school, I guarantee I would be dead or in prison.

How many more young people are dead or in prison because someone in authority wrote them off at a young age? Hopefully not too many, but a great deal are not fulfilling their potential. If you are one of those people, I hope you will take this opportunity to change direction, forget what anyone told you about how much you can achieve, ignore anyone that is still telling you that you can't do it and make it happen for yourself. It is incredibly motivating when you start proving them wrong. Just the belief you can do more and achieve more is often all you need to start taking a leap of faith into some of those opportunities that are in front of you every day.

17. Free Enterprise Works

Napoleon once said that Britain was a nation of shop keepers. In essence he was right; Britain, North America, Australia and most of the English speaking world are living proof that free enterprise works. A huge amount of small businesses thrive in Britain and America that employ only a small amount of people individually, but collectively make up one the biggest employers in the world and creates a massive amount of wealth for those involved. Some of these small businesses have also grown into giant industries and have become some of the most profitable companies internationally.

When I first started writing this book I had no intention of pushing free enterprise or actively encouraging people to start their own businesses, but I feel so passionate about it and found it has been so great for me that I couldn't ignore it. I have been involved in a few business start ups over the last ten years and some were more successful than others but without fail, I earned more money through them than I have doing similar work in a salaried job.

By starting your own business or just by going self employed and working freelance it puts you firmly in the driving seat, in total control of your time, money and most importantly your future.

Going it alone isn't for everyone and you may just be looking to take a leap up the career ladder within a bigger company but keep it in mind for the future because it is important to remember that all the time you are working for someone else, you are only helping to make someone else's dreams come true, not your own. OUR OWN dreams and ambitions should be the most important priorities for us.

If you are looking for a promotion it has been proven that the quickest and easiest way to get a promotion is to look for your bosses position in another company. You can often leapfrog a few rungs on your career ladder by doing this too. If you are worried about being loyal to your employer, DON'T! As I have already mentioned; In most companies if they could make the company more profitable and grow quicker by firing you, do you believe they would think twice about it? No, they wouldn't, they would send you packing straight away, that is the kind of loyalty they are giving you so show them the same in return. If you don't believe this you either work for a very rare employer, you work in the public sector or you are seriously deluding yourself. If you can be more profitable and grow in your career quicker by doing something else then go for it.

Don't depend on others

I have met a few people who have some brilliant ideas and buckets of enthusiasm and who have been involved in their own businesses before but only with other people. There are a certain set of entrepreneurs or business people that just can't seem to do it alone, they often have all the ideas and do the bulk of the work and their business partners just end up being a drain on the business. Inevitably it all breaks down for a combination of issues around this imbalance.

If those bright people could just have the guts to go it completely alone I have no doubt they could make it, but they are scared and want the security of someone else's backing. They don't seem to realise though, that a person's backing comes at a very high price and often it's too high. An accountant who worked with a lot of small to medium sized businesses once said to me "a partnership is a sinking ship". I have to agree I haven't seen very many that work well that are not family related or formed between very long standing friends.

If you have a good idea and you think you can make it happen don't let someone else come along for a free ride, do it yourself. To make great things happen and get the make the greatest returns sometimes you have to take all the risk on your own.

The salesman in all of us

When it comes to free enterprise and depending on your own skills, the overriding skill that comes to my mind is selling. This is something some love and others hate but I believe we are all good at if we want to be.

Remember when you were a kid and you tried to convince your parents it was a good idea to buy you that toy you wanted, or that trip you must go on, or party you HAD to go to? Have you ever convinced your partner that this car is the right one for you because of loads of practical reasons but the real reason you want it is because it's fast or looks good? Have you convinced your mates that a certain holiday destination will be the best one or even which bar to go to on a night out for only one reason and that's just you want to go there, even though you actually have no idea how good it is? This is sales and we are ALL inherently good at it because we have been doing it since we could talk, we just don't realise it.

If you want to get what you want you will need to sell. Sell ideas to investors and bank managers, sell products to customers, sell the property you developed and the list goes on. Don't be scared or put off by this; the only difference between this selling and the selling you do every day and have done every day since you were about two years of age, is that you are selling to people you don't know and not your nearest and dearest which makes us feel nervous sometimes.

Personally I feel much more comfortable selling to people I don't know because if I am stretching the truth a little or if I come across as pushy then who cares? I don't know this person so why am I happier "selling" to the people closest to me but not a total stranger?

Here are some good selling techniques I use:

The best selling technique by far is to ask the potential buyer what it is they are looking for, listen to everything they have to say and then press them for even more information about what they want, then take in all that too. Then proceed to tell them how what you have got fits all their requirements, listing back to them everything they wanted (just worded slightly differently). You might need to adapt things slightly and improvise a bit but it's surprisingly easy to do. You might think this is too basic and transparent and could not work but just try it. I use this technique on an almost daily basis and it works 90% of the time for me. The main key to this is to shut up and listen for the first half of the conversation, resist any temptation to dive in, just take in everything they say and then use it to sell straight back to them.

A mistake a lot of people make is to wait for people to ask questions. I noticed this when I was selling one of my houses and the agent insisted she did all the viewings. After a few viewings I was wondering why we were getting no interest, the house was newly renovated and decorated, it was priced really competitively and it was in a great location. So the next time there was a viewing I made sure I was there to see how the agent was selling the house. What she did was something I have seen many times since and does not work too well (except in a few exceptional circumstances); she showed the potential buyers into the house and then passively pointed them around the house, waiting for them to ask questions. Not a good way to sell at all, people don't like asking questions people like to be told, people often need good the best aspects pointing out to them, they won't always see them. The next time there was a viewing I insisted that I do it. I told them the history of the house, the renovations I had done, the good points about the property and the area, the property's unique features and how nice the neighbours were. They bought the house, the first viewing I did instead of the passive agent and it was sold. Don't wait to be asked questions, lay it all out on a gold platter for them so they can't possibly have any questions or say no. View every prospective purchaser, viewer, investor as the buyer until they state otherwise. Decide in your mind that this is the last potential buyer you will get and this one must buy what you are selling, don't be desperate but be determined.

18. Don't Save, SPEND (or invest)!

When it comes to investing in anything, any idiot can tell you it's about "buying low and selling high" it doesn't take a genius to understand that but it is amazing how few of us apply that simple principle.

When I made the decision to invest in more property and land a few years ago, I could see that the funds I had to invest would not go very far for the type of property I wanted in the area I lived or anywhere near there. It certainly would not have got me close to what I wanted, which was a farm and vineyard. This is when I concentrated on WHAT I wanted and looked very far and wide, even in different countries to find what I wanted for the price I could afford. By looking outside my normal sphere I was not only able to find what I was looking for but it ensured I was buying at the bottom of the market somewhere else, instead of at the top of the market where I was living.

I once believed real money and business only existed in major cities like London where I lived at the time, I am happy to say I have been proved wrong many times since. It can be difficult to do but if you can think outside your psychological and physical boundaries you really can get what you want.

I am terrible at saving money, I can't do it. What's it for? I keep asking myself and how much do I need? If you are just saving for the sake of it, you can't always answer these questions. Now I work like this: What do I want? What do I need? How much are those things going to cost and how can they be achieved? Now I will get the money and make them happen.

Whenever I refer to wealth in this book I am not just talking about money. Money is not as important as people believe; it comes and goes and is a requirement for some of life's essentials and luxuries but is not the be all and end all.

Recently I have been explaining amounts of money earned like this: You could earn a million every day but if it costs a million + 1 to cover your basic daily expenses then you are screwed. When I say this to people I usually get silence. I then go on to say that random amounts of money are not important; however the costs of what you want and the amount of your expenses are important. Concentrate on what you want and what you need and how much they cost and go get it.

People pay regularly into savings for years without knowing why, it's OK to save some money but know what it's for, how much you are trying to achieve and how quickly you can get it. Make it happen! I know this sounds odd to a lot of people but it really works, focus on the things you want and the goals you want to achieve and make them happen, don't get bogged down with amounts of money.

When I set out on my journey to transform my life and get myself out of the hostel I didn't fully understand the concept or value of money, £50 was a fortune to me at that time, £1000 was an unimaginable amount of money. My quest was never about money at the beginning, it did not cross my mind once, my quest was for a better life and to change my life generally for the better not to make money. At some point a few years after that my perspective changed and it became almost all about the money. By approaching success from both angles I can now see that success is harder when you just focus on the money, just raw cash. My life progress slowed considerably at that point. When we start concentrating on just money we lose focus of our goals and our perspective changes.

Money can't buy you happiness but it really helps! Money is important, we can't live without it, certainly not without more guidance than I can provide anyway. A lot of people, in fact most people, will measure success by money, I certainly did for a while. It wasn't until I looked back and realised that money didn't enter my head much when I first started my quest to get out of the homeless hostel.

When I saw my first successes money just followed; I didn't actively pursue it. This was a really important thing for me to learn from my young self, I did spend some time more recently concentrating almost solely on money, the lack of it, how much I was making, how much I wasn't making and how much I was in debt, It was all consuming. I finally realised where I was going wrong, took some tips from myself and stopped worrying about money. I took some simple steps to manage my debt a little better, turned to my new luck and opportunities and gave them my full focus. When I did this the money literally just followed my new successes, not mountains of money but certainly enough to clear my debts, travel, get the car I wanted and generally make life more comfortable. These are the things I want and enjoy. I don't enjoy staring at money or a bank balance, I like having a nice life and that is what I have and what I am continuing to improve.

When this money started flowing in it was tempting to slip back to the money mentality and start thinking "I made this money doing this, now it's time to make some more". I didn't do this, I didn't start counting on more coming in or making grand plans to buy a huge yacht or a Ferrari. I actually did nothing, I took some time off, I only worked the minimum I had to, I spent a lot more time at home with my family. It was great, I really enjoyed that time and it didn't bother me for a second that I could be making more money if I wasn't doing that.

Financial security is important but having excessive piles of money isn't more important than being happy. Quality of life is not measured in pounds or dollars, life isn't all about work either, we are here for a very short space of time and we need to enjoy it more.

I wanted to insert this well known story here because it has a very important message about freedom, happiness and the true meaning of wealth. It illustrates perfectly that a lot of people are chasing money in the belief that it will bring freedom, when freedom is already ours, we just don't realise it.

An American tourist was at the pier of a small coastal Mexican village when a small boat with just one fisherman docked.

Inside the small boat were several large yellow fin tuna. The tourist complimented the Mexican on the quality of his fish and asked how long it took to catch them.

The Mexican replied, "Only a little while."

The tourist then asked, "Why didn't you stay out longer and catch more fish?"

The Mexican said, "With this I have more than enough to support my family's needs."

The tourist then asked, "But what do you do with the rest of your time?"

The Mexican fisherman said, "I sleep late, fish a little, play with my children, take siesta with my wife, Maria, stroll into the village each evening where I sip wine and play guitar with my amigos, I have a full and busy life."

The tourist scoffed, "I can help you. You should spend more time fishing; and with the proceeds, buy a bigger boat: With the proceeds from the bigger boat you could buy more boats. Eventually you would have a fleet of fishing boats. Instead of selling your catch to a middleman you would sell directly to the processor; eventually opening your own cannery. You would control the product, processing and distribution. You could leave this small coastal fishing village and move to Mexico City, then Los Angeles and eventually New York where you could run your ever-expanding enterprise."

The Mexican fisherman asked, "But, how long will this all take?"

The tourist replied, "15 to 20 years."

"But what then?" asked the Mexican.

The tourist laughed and said, "That's the best part. When the time is right you would sell your company stock to the public and become very rich, you would make millions."

"Millions? Then what?"

The American said, "Then you would retire. Move to a small coastal fishing village where you would sleep late, fish a little, play with your kids, take siesta with your wife, stroll to the village in the evenings where you could sip wine and play your guitar with your amigos."

For those already in a fulfilling job:

While finishing this book I started discussing it a lot among friends and posting excerpts on my blog. I perhaps got a bit carried away with the tone of my language encouraging people to set up their own businesses, quit the rat race and become an entrepreneur. A couple of good friends brought me back down to earth and reminded me not everyone hates their jobs and they were fulfilled with the type of work they do.

One of them is a counsellor and key worker helping adults with serious drug and alcohol addiction. I am incredibly proud to call him a friend and someone I went to school with. He loves his job and wants to help the people he works with every day, that is what motivates him and he has a very fulfilling job. However I did point out to him that he could write a book on his experiences to help addicts and other counsellors of addicts. I also suggested he could one day start his own treatment centre where things were done his way and could draw on all of his own experiences. I wanted to show him and others that even though you can do meaningful and fulfilling work that doesn't mean you can't put something personal out in the world too.

19. Remember who you are working for; YOU!

A few years back when considering content for this book I did some quick research on people who hated their jobs. Whilst doing this research one quote I got, one line of advice, stuck in my head and it's a line I have already used earlier in this book: When you are working for someone else, all you are doing is helping someone else's dreams come true. It's so true and it really resonates with me, I tell it to people all the time.

Lots of us often work in jobs we don't really like, for years at a time, often working unpaid overtime, taking calls in our own time when we are at home or on holiday. Why? All we are doing in this situation is quite literally helping someone else achieve their dream while we ignore our own. This doesn't mean that we should all be self employed or set up our own businesses, although I believe it would be fantastic if every person who reads this book starts a successful venture or investment for themselves. We can work for companies AND stay mindful of our own goals. Perhaps you need to keep your eye on that promotion and if you don't get it, get a better job at another company. If it makes more financial development sense for you to take a new job at a different company, even a competitor, then take it. Don't think twice about it because your employers wouldn't if it was the other way round. Those that know me will have already heard me say: You can't be a hero in your own backyard, so you'll probably need to travel somewhere else to show off your greatness. Do not take your eye off the ball though, treat your new job the same, work hard but remember who you are working for, YOU.

While you are carrying out your daily routine, at home or at your place of work, doing what is expected of you, or doing what you are told there are millions of other people not doing what they are told or going through the motions. Right now there are thousands of people sitting on airplanes going to Paris, Rome, Barcelona, Rio (insert other cool destinations here) to promote their own ventures, sipping champagne and the only pressure they feel is from themselves.

I am actually writing this section while sat on a plane from London to Budapest, not drinking champagne and not overly glamorous but it's 14.30 on a regular Tuesday, most people I know are sat in an office, doing a nine to five job they don't really like that much with a boss they don't care for and/or working for a company they don't enjoy working for, with a lot of people they don't like too much. While they are there I am here doing with MY life what I want to do with it. I am here today on this flight because I chose to be and at the time of my choosing. I am not doing what someone else is demanding, I am not having to be somewhere I don't want to be at a time that isn't good for me and I'm not being told off for being ten minutes late, or using the Internet too much or any other ridiculous control some companies and people exercise over others that choose to work for them.

I know this sounds like a bit of a rant but it's what is important to me now in my life. I choose where I go and what I do, how hard I work and how much money I make. It is freedom that I want more than anything and I think that's what most people want, which is why we get obsessed with money because we think it buys freedom. Money can buy freedom to an extent but freedom can also be created and that's what I am doing; cultivating my own freedom.

Recently I gave a friend of mine a lift to Budapest airport when I was working in Hungary. My Hungarian friend lives in Switzerland and he travels back to his native Hungary regularly where he has several properties. He was telling me about when he escaped the Communism in Eastern Europe and made it to Switzerland in 1980; he described total control and oppression by the authorities in Eastern Europe at that time, but he still had a determination to trade and have his own little businesses on the quiet.

After escaping to Switzerland he set up a business renovating and selling cars and trucks, he still does this on a lesser scale. At the end of the conversation he exclaimed so passionately that it is freedom that matters to him most and he would never go back to a situation where someone told him where to be every day, at what time and what he must do when he is there. "What price would it take for me to be told I can't fly to Switzerland today because I have to be at the office or another job?" he said "Or how much would you have to offer me to put someone else in control of my life Monday to Friday? I don't know, probably more than anyone is going to offer me"? The seriousness and conviction on his face and in his eyes mirrored my own when I spoke about these things but what he had been through in his life added more weight to the argument than I could give.

Here is a useful exercise to do, try it now, you might need a calculator (most mobile phones have a calculator function on). I am going to do it with you and for this exercise I am going to pretend I am in one of my old jobs as an IT engineer on a reasonable salary of £35,000.00 per annum.

1. Work out how much you get paid in a day by dividing your annual salary by 365, so for me in my theoretical job it would be £95.89.
2. Now knock off approximately a third, which is about what your tax and other contributions are, so for me that would be about £32 (I did say approximately) so I am left with £63.89.
3. Now take off how much it costs you to travel to work every day, I was travelling 25 miles to work every day so there and back is 50 miles, at a modest cost of £0.25 per mile that would be £12.50, so I am now left with £51.39. If you are unsure of how many miles you travel to and from work check on Google Maps directions, it is often further than you think. If you use public transport it will be easier to work out your exact daily travel costs.
4. Now subtract the cost of additional work clothes you need and extra dry cleaning costs. I had to wear a suit every day and even when I didn't I had to wear smart clothes and shoes that I wouldn't normally wear every

day but I didn't have to wear Armani so I'll minus a modest £3 per day, now I'm left with £48.39.

5. If you buy lunch every day which you wouldn't normally buy if you were working from home (which I did) subtract that off, I spent about £5 a day on deli sandwiches, so now I'm left with £43.39.

6. Now take off any childcare you have to pay for every day, for me that was about £35 per day but I shared that cost with my wife so my share was £17.50, now I'm left with just £25.89.

7. Subtract any other additional expenses you need to pay out just to go to work and allow you to do your job every day, e.g. extra phone calls from your mobile, using your own laptop or home internet. What about unpaid overtime when you are paying additional childcare, parking or other expenses? I'm going to minus a paltry £5 for miscellaneous additional expenses. What figure are you left with?

I am left with £20.89; that is the price of my freedom. Are you selling your freedom on a daily basis for that small amount of money (or less)?

The most important second step of this test is this: Set a date in you diary to go out for lunch this Friday, even if you just eat your lunch on a park bench or in your car. On that Friday lunchtime away from your job, do this exercise again, now divide the final figure in half, that is the amount of money you will get for going back to work that afternoon. My figure for my theoretical job is £10.45! Is it worth it? Think about following your dreams and put a higher price on your freedom!

If you think this calculation is silly then consider that this is the exact type of calculation I or any other businessman, entrepreneur or investor would do to work out if a venture is profitable enough to consider doing. None of the expenses I have added are excessive and every one of them is real and relevant. Your job every day is your venture, your income and your business and you should know what the end profit is and if it is worth for you to do it or not. Your annual salary is your turnover and the figure we have just calculated is your daily profit after expenses. If I multiply the daily profit figure above to give me an annual profit it comes out at £3812.42. Less than four grand!! Are you telling me you couldn't make 4k a year doing something for yourself and are you going to tell me it's worth getting up every day and dealing with all the crap and all the idiots for that small amount of money?

This is how this exercise can work in reverse too, break down the salary into a daily "take home" amount by doing the exercise above and now ask yourself: Could I make that money more easily doing something else? Could you make that money by turning your hobby into a business, can you make something that others would pay for, write a book and impart some of your knowledge, invest in property, use your existing skills to go freelance, are you good at restoring furniture or cars that you could sell for a profit? The list goes on and the tax system is usually on your side if you are self employed or run a business, definitely more so than being employed and having an inflated amount of tax and deductions extracted from your salary before you even see it every month.

My grandfather died just before I started writing this book and some of the things he said to me in the months before he passed away have really stuck in my mind and I have gone over them several times in my head. One of the things he told me was not to have any regrets and to make sure I do all the worthwhile things I could dream of.

The most poignant and memorable thing he explained to me was his deep regret that he never started his own business or at least tried being self employed. With a slight tear in his eye he admitted he was a little envious that I had struck out on my own and I answered only to myself. I think it's incredibly sad that at eighty six years old and close to death he had such huge regrets. He worked for the same family for over fifty years, doing pretty much the same job day in and day out from fifteen years old to retirement at sixty five.

It really made me wonder why we do the same things for years on end even though we dream of something different. I have been guilty of it at times but I make sure I shake myself out every so often and question whether I am following my dreams or not or if I am challenging myself enough. Don't think your life will last forever because it won't, don't believe you will be fit and healthy forever because you won't. I am not trying to be negative or depressing, I am really not, quite the opposite. I am trying to make people see things as I do and make the most of life instead of wasting it. What will your legacy be, what will people remember you for when you are gone or will you just be another anonymous tax payer?

Seizing the day (Carpe Diem) is a positive thing, do something crazy today, quit your job and start that business you always wanted or go freelance or buy that run down house in Portugal you dreamt about. It might seem nuts but do it now, don't waste another day of your precious life. It might not work out how you expect it to but you have to start somewhere, you can always change the plan later on. To move forward you have to actually move, sometimes sideways, occasionally backwards a bit but if you stand still then you go nowhere. Make a move today, I dare you!

For more information on tips, seminars, courses and more books by Matt Kinsella go to:

www.mattkinsella.com

Printed in Great Britain
by Amazon.co.uk, Ltd.,
Marston Gate.